GHOSTS
AND THE SPIRIT WORLD

GHOSTS

AND THE SPIRIT WORLD

True cases of hauntings and visitations from the
earliest records to the present day

Paul Roland

ARCTURUS

ARCTURUS

This edition published in 2014 by Arcturus Publishing Limited
26/27 Bickels Yard, 151–153 Bermondsey Street,
London SE1 3HA

ISBN: 978-1-78212-278-4
AD002725UK

Printed in China

CONTENTS

INTRODUCTION

LOTS of people have seen a ghost – at least that's the impression I got as soon as friends and acquaintances learned I was writing another ghost book and looking for real-life experiences that had not already appeared in print. If they hadn't seen a ghost themselves, they knew someone who had. While hearsay evidence can't be considered in a serious study of the subject, the number of stories attested to a compelling prima facie case for the existence of restless spirits, ghosts, poltergeists and all manner of paranormal phenomena. A typical example of a ghostly encounter was told to me by a friend who assured me that the witness was sceptical and pragmatic, the last person who would admit to the possibility of life after death. The witness had awoken in the night and gone to the bathroom, but she couldn't bring herself to cross the threshold. The door was open, but some intangible presence was preventing her from going in. While she told herself she was being irrational, that there was nothing to fear, she still couldn't muster the courage to enter the room. She called her husband, who was usually contemptuous of the supernatural, but he too couldn't bring himself to go in. Feeling somewhat ridiculous, but increasingly anxious, they began throwing things at the open door, hoping to dispel the 'force' they sensed was obstructing the entrance. By now the hair on the back of their necks was prickling and they had no doubt that this was a malign presence. They spent the night in another part of the house, sleeping fitfully until morning. The next day, when they visited the bathroom, they sensed that whatever had terrorized them had departed.

The couple had spent a small fortune renovating the house and converting an old barn in the grounds into bed-and-breakfast apartments for holiday-makers. However, they couldn't shrug off the oppressive feeling that clung to them like a damp cloth. They made up their minds that morning to sell and start again somewhere else.

During the sale, they learned that the barn had been the site of a suicide many years earlier. The former owner of the house had kept a horse and wagon in a stall where the bathroom now was; one night, he climbed on to the cart and hanged himself from a wooden beam.

The reason I believe my friend's story is that the couple concerned were his parents, who were by nature suspicious of anyone who claimed to have encountered paranormal phenomena. They never experienced anything of that kind again and remained stubbornly sceptical of all things supernatural for the rest of their lives.

THE MISSING STEPS

The same friend told me about another couple who had converted an old property. After moving in, they were kept awake by what sounded like footsteps on the wooden staircase approaching their bedroom. These noises always occurred at the same time each night, so the lady of the house decided to count the number of stairs to see if they corresponded with the number of footsteps she could hear. The next night, she counted twelve footsteps and, as there were only ten stairs, she put the sound down to noisy plumbing and ignored the nightly disturbance from then on. But a couple of years later, when builders ripped up the staircase to make alterations, they discovered that there were two additional steps on the original stone stairwell beneath the modern wooden staircase!

Other people told me in confidence of paranormal experiences that had shaken their beliefs – encounters that presumably would have remained unrecorded had I not encouraged the witnesses to share them with me. They seemed almost relieved to talk about their experiences and recollected them vividly. It was as though the encounters had happened the day before, so strong was the impression they had made.

THE DISAPPEARING NUN

A typical example occurred off-air when I was giving a BBC radio interview on a totally unrelated subject. Picking up on something in a biography I had written, in which the subject of the book had foretold his own early death (a prediction which came to pass), the presenter told me of a time when she was hospitalized with a life-threatening illness. One night she woke in a highly emotional state. A nun on the ward came over to calm her and sat and talked quietly for some considerable time until the patient fell asleep. When the woman woke in the early hours, she asked a nurse if she could talk to the nun again as the night shift hadn't ended and she thought the nun must still be on duty. The nurse had no knowledge of any nun and no one else at the hospital recalled ever having seen a nun in the building. 'I'm getting a shiver just thinking about it,' the presenter told me. 'And I can still see her now as if she was here just a moment ago.'

Often the encounter with benign or malevolent spirits is fleeting, but the impact on the individual who experiences a brief brush with the dead will last a lifetime. A middle-aged man told me that two days after the death of his father he felt the old man's spirit brush past him as he entered the living room of the family home. There was no overwhelming sensation of love or reassurance that some people experience when they are visited by a recently deceased relative, nor was there a feeling of fear. There was nothing, only the sense of a presence passing from the house and the certainty that it was his father. It lasted only a moment or two, but from that day the son hasn't questioned whether or not there is life after death.

THE INEBRIATED SPIRIT

It's particularly gratifying for a ghost-hunter to hear a converted sceptic describe the experience which compelled him or her to question a lifelong conviction that there is no such thing as a ghost. A musician I know, who is as down to earth as they come, described the day when he and a few friends were messing around with an Ouija board in their last year of secondary school. He had recently witnessed a fatal accident near his home: an acquaintance had died while driving under the influence of alcohol. My friend began by asking the Ouija board questions about his own family, to which only he knew the answer. To make sure that he was not guiding the upturned glass unconsciously, he took his finger off it. His questions were answered correctly – but there was something unusual in the spelling, with extra letters as if the words were slurred. On a hunch, my friend asked if the spirit moving the glass was the person who had recently died while drunk at the wheel, and the answer given was 'Yes'. Just to rule out the possibility that his friends might be moving the glass, he asked them to turn their palms upwards and place the tips of their fingernails on the base, so that they could not move the glass by themselves. And it still moved in answer to his questions.

Soon after this impromptu séance, my friend was offered a reading by a young woman who happened to mention that she was psychic. During the reading she became distressed as she described a young man who had been deeply depressed by his failing business. She also complained of a dull pain in her neck. It transpired that someone close to my friend had recently hanged himself and his body had been discovered by his children, a scene the psychic described in some detail. The information she picked up concerning the problems with his business was also accurate.

The most compelling evidence for the existence of ghosts is that supplied by independent witnesses and all the better if the witness happens to be a pillar of the community. A Polish friend told me of the day a relative of hers went to the local cemetery to visit the grave of her daughter, who had died young. The weather was dreadful, but she braved the rain and biting wind.

When she had paid her respects and said her prayers for the dead, she turned to leave, but was stopped by a priest who had been watching her from a window of the church. He saw how wet and cold she was and invited her in for a hot drink. Before she went on her way, the bereaved woman began to speak about her daughter, but the priest stopped her, saying: 'I saw her. She was standing next to you the whole time.'

PHANTOM ARMS

An appeal for true ghost stories from my foreign friends brought this chilling tale from Per Faxneld of Stockholm University.

'When my wife's paternal grandmother, Elsie, was young, she and her husband Stig rented a summerhouse in the Stockholm archipelago. It was located on a fairly big island named Singö. Elsie and Stig took it for the whole summer for several years, and were very fond of the place. It was an old wooden house, located next to a smithy from the late 1700s. According to locals, the smithy was haunted. There don't appear to have been any specific legends attached to it, no demonic blacksmith who made a pact with the devil or such, but people heard strange sounds coming from the building: a hammer beating on an anvil and a creaking wheelbarrow being pushed around in the middle of the night, in spite of the smithy not having been in use for several generations.

'Stig, who passed away a few years ago, was a very level-headed working-class person. The same goes for Elsie, although she possesses a more artistic temperament and is a talented amateur painter. Elsie occasionally heard the mystifying sounds, but was not too bothered by them. After a few summers on Singö, however, something much more frightening occurred. One afternoon my father-in-law, Lars-Olof, then a few months old, was sleeping in his cradle while Elsie was cooking in the kitchen. Stig was absent. When Elsie entered the bedroom to check on her son, she saw something that truly terrified her – a pair of arms coming out of the wooden wall and reaching for little Lars-Olof in the cradle! She screamed, ran over to her boy, grabbed him and fled the house. Upon his return, Elsie told Stig what she had seen, but he was sceptical – although he had heard, and would later again hear, the hammering and the wheelbarrow.

'Lars-Olof grew up, unharmed by the attempt by the ghost to steal him away, and during one of his summers on Singö as a teenager met and fell in love with my mother-in-law, Anette, whose family had built a summerhouse of their own on the island. She and Lars-Olof would both hear the ghostly sounds at times, but neither witnessed anything as shocking as the grasping apparitional arms.

To this day, Elsie maintains the whole thing happened exactly as she has always said it did. The family still spend their summers on Singö, but neither my wife nor I have ever seen or heard anything while staying there.'

IN THE PARTY SPIRIT

Having explored many aspects of the paranormal and written several books on the subject, I thought I had a good understanding of such phenomena. I had my beliefs, based largely on personal experience and on those of psychics and mediums I had worked with, but I also had my doubts about other aspects, specifically spirit photography. Until, that is, a member of my family happened to mention seeing a photograph her teenage daughter had taken at a children's birthday party in 2005. It was passed around the group of friends, all of whom remarked on the presence of a little girl in Victorian dress who could be seen peeping out from under the legs of one of the children. This was not the typical faint, blurry image one associates with alleged 'ghost photographs', but a sharp, unmistakable image of a little girl with blonde ringlets. Yet nobody could identify her.

It was a small party in a private house, so there was no chance for an uninvited guest to sneak in unnoticed. Everyone in the photograph knew one another, with the exception of the unidentified child. Even more remarkably, as the photograph was being taken one of the children ran screaming from the room and had to be comforted by her mother. It wasn't until the photograph was developed that the hosts understood the reason for her fear – she must have seen the ghost.

So I no longer dismiss the possibility of such phenomena out of hand, although I maintain a healthy scepticism with regard to some of the more dramatic claims.

AN APPARITION'S APPROVAL

While I have had many paranormal encounters, such as out-of-body experiences and an awareness of the physical presence of spirits, I did not actually see a ghost until 2004. That year I began recording a new album after a seven-year absence from the music business; but I was uncertain whether I should return to music or devote my energies to writing more books. As I stood in the control room listening to the playback of a song, I saw the ghost of the person who had initially inspired me just a foot away from me. I had not been thinking of him and the music did not resemble his own, so his spontaneous appearance took me completely by surprise. He was smiling gently as if giving me his approval and he remained as large as life and as clear as my sound engineer, who was also present. Once I had realized the purpose of his appearance, he faded from view. This story illustrates my theory that if a ghost appears when we least expect it, this tends to rule out the possibility that it could be a figment of our imagination.

AUNTIE IS DEAD, DEAR

One morning in 2006 I was startled out of my sleep by the unmistakable voice of an aunt of mine, as clear as if she had been in the room with me. 'Auntie R— is dead, dear.' Normally when we 'hear' a voice in our head it is our own, but on this occasion it was definitely my aunt's voice, one I couldn't imitate if I tried, speaking in a matter-of-fact manner as if telling me that it was time for breakfast.

I phoned my mother and gently suggested it might be a good idea to check up on my aunt as she was frail and on her own, her husband having been admitted to hospital. My mother called and received no reply. When the hospital confirmed that my aunt had not been to visit her husband recently, my mother contacted the police. They went to the flat and, unable to raise a response, broke down the door and found my aunt unconscious. She had suffered a rupture in her brain, but had been found just in time and after an operation made a good recovery.

Why she had communicated with me and not my mother (who is also psychic) I don't know, and why she didn't manifest to warn me I can't say either. However, I believe that ghosts and other related phenomena are projections of the essence of an individual and we perceive them according to our current state of mind and level of sensitivity, just as a radio or TV can be tuned to various frequencies. As the stories in this book suggest, it appears that an individual's level of awareness at a given moment is what is crucial. It determines the form in which they receive the communication, be it a vivid dream, a disembodied voice or a vision in their mind's eye (the Third Eye of psychic sight), which evaporates as soon as they snap back to consciousness.

So if you are fascinated by the paranormal and would like to develop your own innate psychic sensitivity, don't be afraid to explore the spirit world in the safety of a psychic development or healing circle, for like attracts like, and the experiences can only enlarge your understanding of the universe and the greater reality of which we are all a part. After twenty years of studying, practising and teaching psychic development, I have come to understand that the supernatural is an extension of the natural world and is governed by the same universal laws, not contrary to them.

However, reckless dabbling in the occult just for fun can be dangerous. Communicating with discarnate spirits using an Ouija board, or exploring haunted houses and derelict 'lunatic asylums' with the expectation of rooting out the resident spooks, is as risky as venturing into a jungle and beating the undergrowth with a stick in the hope of luring out the inhabitants.

RELIGION AND THE SUPERNATURAL

It is significant and revealing that the word 'ghost' (derived from the Old Norse 'geisa', meaning 'to rage' or 'to terrify') simply means 'soul' or 'spirit' in Old English ('gaast'), implying that in olden times an apparition was considered a natural phenomenon. The word 'ghost' only acquired a more sinister meaning after the failure of the Crusades in the 14th century, when the Church struggled to resist the tide of change questioning its authority. Orthodox Christianity has always considered ghosts to be evil spirits who take the form of the deceased in order to deceive the living. Acknowledging the existence of ghosts would have been in conflict with the Christian concept of the afterlife, in which all souls go either to heaven or hell and the only disembodied spirits are those of the saints.

1

PHANTOMS IN PHOTOS

In the second half of the 19th century, the North American city of Boston was buzzing with talk of technological advances that promised to transform it into a modern metropolis to rival New York and Washington, D. C. The First Transcontinental Railroad would soon link the Eastern Seaboard with California to unite a nation that was still in mourning after five years of civil war.

Meanwhile, inventions such as electricity and the telegraph promised a life of faster communication and greater comfort and convenience. Into this heady whirl of progress and expectation emerged the new science of photography, greeted as a modern miracle in an age still dependent on horse-drawn transport, gas street lighting and dirt roads.

Sadly, the remarkable inventions of the age gave scant comfort to grieving families for whom the recent conflict was still a lingering presence. Many could not accept that they would never see their fathers, sons and brothers again. While some people took solace in religion, others sought reassurance in the flourishing Spiritualist movement that offered them the possibility of communicating with the dear departed, however briefly. It also, inevitably, exposed them to the risk of being fleeced by conmen and unscrupulous individuals posing as genuine mediums.

Boston photographer William Mumler did not set out to prey on the bereaved by promising to capture

23

the spirit of their loved ones on film, but he saw how eagerly they queued at his studio to have their portraits taken and how willingly they handed over $10 for the privilege. Few complained that he charged five times more than his competitors, but then no one else offered their clients the possibility of a 'reunion' with their deceased loved ones that could be photographed for posterity.

In 1861, while developing a plate in his darkroom, Mumler, a former jewellery engraver, had chanced on what appeared to be a new phenomenon, 'spirit photography'. The photo he was working on was a self-portrait, but it had a blemish of some kind which, when printed and examined in daylight, was revealed to be the likeness of a young girl. Mumler showed it to a friend as a curiosity and joked that the mysterious figure was that of his dead cousin. To his astonishment, his friend assumed he was serious and urged him to send the photo to a leading Spiritualist publication, the *Banner of Light*, which duly published it as irrefutable evidence that spirits could be seen by the new science. Photography was still a relative mystery to the general public, who assumed that the camera recorded only what it saw. Photographic phenomena, effects and tricks of the light were then unknown. Few people considered that the picture might be a fake or an accidental double exposure.

A BOOMING BUSINESS

Whatever misgivings Mumler might have entertained at the thought of conning the public and profiting from their grief were cast aside when he saw the busy waiting room at his Washington Street studio in the days following the picture's publication. His wife Hannah, a clairvoyant, didn't need much persuading to aid him in the deception. She engaged the clients in small talk while they waited their turn and then passed on the information to her husband, so that he could make his performance behind the camera more convincing. He was the 'channel' for the spirits and his wife was the medium who drew them from the world beyond. But there was no guarantee that the dead would comply. Often clients would leave with only a conventional family portrait and the hope that the deceased would put in an appearance at a subsequent sitting – for another $10. In this way, the couple ensured themselves a regular and substantial income for a minimal outlay.

Mumler's rivals were not so naïve, however, and were incensed that he was turning their profession into a freakshow. They had their suspicions about how he achieved his phantom effects, but proving them was another matter. The whole affair was complicated by the fact that fake phantom photography had become a fashionable business, with stereoscopic cards of 'ghosts' and 'devils' being offered for the amusement of the middle classes, who purchased them as a novelty item.

In his autobiography, Mumler described how a competitor, James Black, wagered $50 that he could expose the phantom photographs as fakes. However, after examining the camera and watching Mumler develop the plates, Black admitted he had failed to find anything suspicious. Mumler claimed he had even converted the sceptic, who left the studio muttering, 'My God! Is it possible?' But we only have Mumler's version of events.

In 1863, Mumler invited Dr Child, a Philadelphia physician, to study his methods and put an end to the growing rumours that the phenomenon was nothing more than an effect achieved by double exposure, trick lenses, reflections or concealed accomplices dressed as 'apparitions'. The latter was a favourite trick of fraudsters, who capitalized on the fact that their sitters were required to remain absolutely still while the shutter remained open for up to a minute. This gave ample time for assistants to appear and disappear, leaving a ghostly impression on the plate.

CLOSER INSPECTION

Dr Child accepted the challenge and visited the Boston studio with several friends who oversaw the entire process, from the preparation of the plates to the developing of the prints. They also examined the equipment and made a thorough search of the studio for compartments where an accomplice could be hidden. To eliminate the chance that the plates might be switched at some stage, Dr Child marked each of them with a diamond but still Mumler produced his phantom portraits, to the astonishment of the sceptics.

Yet the doubters would not be persuaded. That same year the physician, poet and essayist Oliver Wendell Holmes Snr. wrote a damning exposé of spirit photography in the influential magazine *The Atlantic Monthly*. He poured scorn on those who were duped into accepting such images as genuine as well as those who fabricated them for profit.

As a result of the article, Mumler's clients took a closer look at their precious 'evidence'. Several of them realized that there was something suspiciously familiar in the faint impressions, which bore a striking similarity to photographs of their loved ones taken while they were alive. Prominent Spiritualists who had previously greeted the photographs with enthusiasm also began to question their authenticity, and were forced to examine their faith in the movement when told that several of the 'spirits' were very much alive and well and living in Boston!

Mumler didn't protest his innocence, but quietly left town. In 1868 he set up business on Broadway. Evidently, news of his chicanery hadn't filtered through to New York, where he enjoyed a roaring trade, encouraged by a flair for shameless self-publicity. 'It is now some eight years since I commenced to take these remarkable pictures,' he boasted, 'and thousands... bear testimony to the truthful likeness of their spirit friends they have received through my mediumistic power.'

Mumler was prone to exaggeration, but it is estimated that he must have taken around 500 photographs by this time, which, at $10 a sitting, amounted to a considerable sum. But his satisfaction was shortlived – in March 1869 several members of the Photographic Section of the American Institute of the City of New York took their suspicions to the press and demanded an investigation into his activities.

BROUGHT TO COURT

A few weeks later, Joseph Tooker, an undercover police officer posing as a grieving client, paid for a portrait with a deceased relative. When Mumler failed to produce the goods, Tooker arrested him and threw him into the notorious city prison known as the 'Tombs'.

Incredibly, when Mumler emerged to stand trial on 21 April, he found the courtroom packed with Spiritualists offering moral support to the man they felt had produced irrefutable evidence validating their beliefs. It was clear from the hostile and mocking tone adopted by the press that it was not only Mumler on trial, but the Spiritualist movement itself. The *New York Times* poured scorn on the women who packed the public gallery and filled the court 'with a cold and clammy atmosphere… worn down [by] ethereal essences'. Other publications declared Mumler 'a stupendous fraud'.

But if the prosecution thought they had ample evidence to convict, they were mistaken. Tooker's testimony was soon overwhelmed by a series of defence witnesses who swore on oath that Mumler had provided them with proof of life after death. One of the most convincing was Charles Livermore, who identified the spectral image in a photograph as that of his late wife. He declared that several of his friends were also prepared to testify to the fact. 'I went there with my eyes open, as a sceptic,' he told the court. He had even tried to put Mumler to the test by arriving a day early for his sitting to foil any preparations the photographer might have been making to produce the desired effect. During the sitting he altered his pose in order to 'defeat any arrangement he might have made… I was on the lookout all the while'. For those unable to attend the trial, *Harper's Weekly* published two photographs of

Livermore and his 'wife' in the 8 May edition and invited its readers to examine them and decide for themselves.

Perhaps the most dramatic testimony was given by a former justice of the New York Supreme Court, Judge John Edmonds, who confessed that he communed with the dead during murder trials. He claimed that they provided him with details of how they had died and whether or not the accused had done the foul deed. Judge Edmonds was in no doubt that Mumler's photographs were genuine.

A HOLLOW VICTORY

Sensing defeat, the prosecution called several photographic experts to the stand to explain how the effects might have been produced. One of them observed that the Livermore 'ghost' cast a shadow, which no ethereal phantom should do. Furthermore, the shadow was cast in the opposite direction to that of the living subject, indicating that there were two separate light sources and that two separate pictures had been taken at different times of the day. The conflicting shadows could not possibly have been cast at the same time.

To conclude, the prosecution called the celebrated carnival showman P.T. Barnum, who boasted that he knew a conman when he saw one. The accused had allegedly sold Barnum a collection of spirit photographs which the showman had put on display in his museum of curiosities. The merchandise had come with an incriminating letter in which Mumler had admitted faking the photographs – or so Barnum claimed, for he had lost the letter in a fire and was unable to produce it to prove his story.

On 3 May Mumler took the stand and asserted, 'I have never used any trick or device, or availed myself of any deception or fraud.' Following this, the defence summed up by implying that the case was nothing less than a witch hunt – Mumler was being persecuted for his 'faith', just as Galileo had been persecuted by the Catholic Church.

Judge Dowling was not persuaded and declared he was convinced that Mumler had defrauded his clients – but as the prosecution had not proven how the deception had been achieved, he had no choice but to set the photographer free.

It was a hollow victory, however, for Mumler was now deep in debt and unable to pay his legal bills. He returned to Boston to live as a lodger with his mother-in-law and there carried on his work, defiantly claiming that he alone could capture the spirits of the deceased on camera. He died in 1884, reviled by the photographic profession which accused him of bringing the new science into disrepute, and after having destroyed his entire archive of negatives, presumably in an effort to remove the evidence of his deception.

PHOTOGRAPH OF A PRESIDENT

If Mumler was a fraud, he was also later seen as a significant figure in the history of photography. He is now credited with several innovations (which he patented), including Mumler's Process, which enabled photographs to be reproduced in publications with no loss of detail. In spite of his sullied reputation as a spirit photographer, his photographs are still of historical interest. His most famous photograph, taken in his cramped Boston studio in 1871, shows an elderly woman dressed in mourning. But the photo also shows her 'husband' standing behind her, his hands resting on her shoulders. The lady's name was Mary Todd Lincoln and the apparition was the late president, Abraham Lincoln. Mary had unmasked several fake mediums, but she had recently been to a séance where her dead husband had communed with her and she wanted to have her photograph taken in the hope that he might appear again. A staunch believer in Spiritualism, she accepted the 'evidence' of the photograph without question, but to the trained eye it is clearly a fake.

THE FACE IS LIKE THAT OF A DEAD PERSON

Around the time that Mumler was defending his battered reputation in a New York court, an English photographer was attracting attention across the Atlantic by claiming to produce similar phenomena. Unlike Mumler, Frederick Hudson had the backing of a respected medium, Mrs Guppy, whose ringing endorsement guaranteed him a steady stream of clients who would not look too closely at his pictures. But others were not so willing to suspend disbelief, among them professional photographer John Beattie, who persuaded Hudson to participate in a controlled experiment and to consent to the results being published in the *British Journal of Photography*.

Hudson's garden studio was a large converted greenhouse, which also served as his darkroom. After the camera equipment and plates were examined, Hudson seated himself with his profile to the camera while his daughter stood next to him, acting as medium. The first photograph showed nothing unusual, but for the second portrait the girl retreated to the background and this time a third seated figure appeared on the print.

'The figure is in a three-quarter position – in front of me, but altogether between me and the background,' Beattie later wrote. 'The figure is draped in black, with a white coloured plaid over the head, and is like both a brother and a nephew of mine. This last point I do not press because the face is like that of a dead person and under lighted.'

A third photograph produced another apparition, 'a standing female figure, clothed in a black skirt, and having a white-coloured, thin linen drapery something like a shawl pattern, upon her shoulders, over which a mass of black hair loosely hung. The figure is in front of me and, as it were, partially between me and the camera.'

Beattie still had his doubts about the authenticity of the images, but he couldn't figure out how Hudson had achieved the results. However, there was one explanation he hadn't considered, perhaps because it was just too simple. Hudson had switched the plates. Such a trick must have aroused suspicion among critics within the Spiritualist movement, because in September 1872 they began voicing their doubts in the pages of the *Spiritualist* magazine, accusing Hudson of double-printing two separate plates or preparing his plates in advance. They cited a photograph in which the pattern of a carpet could be seen superimposed over the fabric of a sitter's clothing, an anomaly that could only have occurred if the carpet had been on the first exposure with the fake spirit.

By this time, the pages of the 'yellow press' were full of sensational exposés of fraudulent mediums and their theatrical parlour tricks. The favourite manifestation was ectoplasm, a dense misty miasma said to indicate the presence of a ghostly spirit. To achieve this effect, a roll of cheesecloth would be teased out of the medium's mouth or dropped down from the ceiling on a string at the climax of the séance.

GENUINE PHOTOGRAPHS

In the 1890s, just as spirit photography looked as though it had lost all credibility, support came from a most unexpected source. J. Traill Taylor, editor of the *British Journal of Photography,* published a series of articles in which he and his staff revealed how certain ghostly effects could be achieved, but they also suggested that some photographs may have been genuine after all. Using a stereoscopic camera to prove his theory, Taylor discovered that 'genuine' images remained two-dimensional and, he argued, they would not have done so had they been faked double exposures.

The following year, Alfred Wallace, co-creator of the theory of evolution, also came to the defence of Spiritualism and spirit photography, arguing along the same lines as Taylor. Just because many photographs were obvious fakes, he wrote, it did not mean that they all were, and consequently photos of dubious veracity should be examined scientifically.

ONE LAST LOOK ROUND

One example of a 'genuine' spirit photo deserving of serious study is commonly known as the 'Lord Combermere Photograph'. Taken in 1891 by amateur photographer Sybell Corbett in the library of Combermere Abbey, Cheshire, it appears to show the faint, glowing figure of a man seated in what Sybell swore had been an empty chair. The exposure was made during the course of an hour and Sybell, who was staying in the house at the time, went to great lengths to ensure no one entered the room while the picture was being taken. The servants would not have dared to sit in the chair, even if they had managed to sneak in. Besides, there was no question as to the chair's occupant; the family and servants identified the figure as Lord Combermere himself. The only problem was that his Lordship was being interred in the family vault at the same time as the picture was being taken. But perhaps the fact that the photograph was taken on the day of his funeral only adds to the validity of the image. What better time for a ghost to take one last look round his ancestral home?

PHOTOGRAPHING
THE INVISIBLE

In the first decade of the new century, many other inexplicable photographs were published in the mainstream press as well as in Spiritualist periodicals – so many, in fact, that books began to appear on the subject. The first bestseller was *Photographing the Invisible* (1911) by James Coates, which made a compelling case for the camera as the new medium for preserving fleeting appearances of the recently deceased. The book was such a success that it was republished ten years later in a considerably expanded edition and is thought to have prompted a series of rigorously scientific experiments devised and monitored by American photographer Charles Cook.

In 1916, Cook put two 'spirit photographers', Edward Wyllie and Alex Martin, to the test, providing them with his own plates and insisting that the negatives be developed by a commercial studio to prevent deception. Cook was convinced that the images the two men produced were genuine and that their rare psychic faculties had helped to conduct the spirit's etheric energy on to the photographic plates. For this reason, he preferred to call the results 'psychic photography', a term that suggested the phenomenon was attributable to the mediumistic abilities of the photographer rather than the camera. His theory was supported by Columbia University's Professor James Hyslop, who endorsed the publication of Cook's study with an enthusiastic introduction that attracted interest from within the academic establishment.

Among the most notable studies was the one undertaken by the eminent British chemist Sir William Crookes of the Royal Society, himself a keen amateur photographer. Sir William spent several years examining all the evidence he could accrue and came to the conclusion that much of what he had seen supported the case for psychic phenomena and spirit photography. However, the more frequently he affirmed his beliefs, the greater the scorn he suffered from colleagues, who accused him of being a credulous eccentric who had lost sight of his scientific principles.

A CONFESSION

Matters were not helped by the activities of the Crewe Circle in the 1920s. William Hope, their de facto leader, made great show of offering prospective clients the opportunity to provide their own photographic plates; however, no one seemed suspicious when he demanded that they leave them in his studio overnight so that they could be 'magnetized' to make them more sensitive to etheric presences!

Hope was frequently accused of fraud and sleight of hand – primarily swapping plates during the handing out of hymn books – but he was never caught. However, he once admitted to Archbishop Thomas Colley, a fervent believer in the supernatural, that he had doctored his photographs. Hope claimed to be a medium and boasted that he could channel the spirit of the Archbishop's late mother; but he mistakenly used the wrong image on the plate and confessed to the deception in an attempt to avoid prosecution. To his relief, the Archbishop was more than charitable, declaring that the old woman in the photograph was indeed his mother. Colley even put a notice in the local paper, inviting those who remembered his mother to call at the rectory to identify her from a selection of photographs that included Hope's 'mistake'. Eighteen people duly confirmed that the unknown woman was the Archbishop's mother, and the incident provided Hope with much-welcome publicity as well as an enthusiastic new patron.

After losing his son and brother in the Great War, the novelist Arthur Conan Doyle had become a convert to the Spiritualist cause. He sprang to Hope's defence after the celebrated ghost-hunter, Harry Price, questioned the veracity of several of Hope's photographs. Price and Conan Doyle were friends, sharing a passion for the paranormal and maintaining an affectionate rivalry, but the heated dispute over Hope's claim to be a genuine medium blighted their relationship. Years later, it came to light that a member of Hope's circle had found a flash lamp and cut-out faces with which the 'medium' had produced his effects. Had this been known at the time, Doyle and Price may have remained friends and Hope would have been exposed.

A MAGICIAN AMONG THE SPIRITS

Another of Conan Doyle's fellow seekers was the celebrated escapologist and illusionist Harry Houdini. It is not generally known that Houdini began his career as a fake medium. However, he soon realized how dishonourable the practice was when he lost a close member of his family and yearned for genuine contact with the deceased. Ashamed of his own small part in the 'great deception', Houdini began a comprehensive investigation and in 1924 published his damning conclusions in a book called *A Magician Among the Spirits*. He had attended countless séances and considered none of them to be genuine; he went on to produce a rational explanation for every form of spectral manifestation he had witnessed, including table rapping, automatic writing and apports (the manifestation of physical objects). His enthusiastic debunking of the paranormal did not endear him to Conan Doyle and others who refused to have their unshakable faith questioned.

Compelling evidence against spirit photography was

mounting and deception was becoming more difficult. The public were generally less gullible than they had been during the height of the Spiritualist craze and the various tricks and crude effects that had been perpetrated upon them were now widely known and easier to identify.

THE BROWN LADY
AND OTHERS

Almost a century later, the photographs that survived scrutiny remain tantalizing glimpses of a new frontier of paranormal research. One such example was the 'Brown Lady of Raynham Hall'. This apparition is remarkable not only because it has defied rational explanation since the picture was taken in September 1936 by *Country Life* photographer Captain Hubert Provand, but also because his assistant, Indre Shira, actually saw the ghost descending the staircase. Shira had urged Provand to take the picture, which duly depicted what the assistant described ('a vapour form which gradually assumed the shape of a woman in a veil'). Provand admitted that he hadn't noticed anything at the time, which suggests that Shira was the more psychically sensitive of the two (assuming, of course, that the photograph is not a fake). Both men were considered reliable witnesses, not given to practical jokes. The ghost is thought to be

Lady Dorothy Walpole, who died in 1726 of a broken neck caused by being pushed down the staircase by her husband after he learned of her affair with another man. She is known as 'the Brown Lady' because her spirit has been seen on several occasions wearing a brown brocade dress.

Between the wars, many supposed 'spirit photographs' were subjected to examination by experts at the leading photographic equipment manufacturer Kodak, who presumably knew a fake when they saw one. Even they failed to find evidence of natural phenomena or fraud in some of the photographs they were asked to assess. There was also the testimony of witnesses who appeared to have nothing to gain from deceiving the public and everything to lose if exposed. Three of the most famous phantom photographs of the post-war years were taken by men of the cloth. The first of these was a colour picture taken by the Reverend R.S. Blance in 1959 at Corroboree Rock in the Australian outback, 160 km (100 miles) from Alice Springs. The site was said to be the location of Native Australian rituals involving animal sacrifice. The photograph shows a translucent woman emerging from the bush. Reverend Blance was not aware of anyone else in the area at the time.

The second photograph, taken in the 1960s by the Reverend K.F. Lord, captures a hooded figure on the steps of the altar at Newby Church in Yorkshire, England. Reverend Lord stated that he didn't see anything at the time and was only photographing the empty sanctuary for his album.

The third image, commonly known as 'the Greenwich Ghost', was snapped in 1966 by a Canadian cleric, the Reverend R.W. Hardy at Queen's House, Greenwich, London. It shows a shrouded figure ascending the Grand Tulip Staircase. All three photographs were scrutinized by experts who assumed them to be fakes, but who subsequently ruled out the possibility of a hoax, a reflection or flaws in the camera or on the film.

THE PHANTOM PASSENGER

A typical photograph that defied explanation was taken by Mrs Mabel Chimney in 1959. Mrs Chimney was visiting her mother's grave in an English churchyard when she decided to photograph it; she then took a separate photo of her husband who was waiting in the car. Although he was alone in the vehicle at the time, the print clearly shows the ghostly presence of an elderly woman in the back seat. The couple identified the mystery woman as Mabel's late mother and offered both the print and the negative to experts at a national newspaper, who declared themselves satisfied that neither had been tampered with.

However, one respected expert, Dr Eric John Dingwall (1890–1986), who devoted sixty years of his life to studying the paranormal as an author and chief researcher for the Society of Psychical Research, remained unconvinced. Dingwall was a firm believer in ghosts and other paranormal phenomena, but he had found fault or fakery in almost every spirit photograph he was asked to examine. When he could not discern any fault, he contended that there must be a rational explanation even if he couldn't provide one. Dingwall's suspicions cannot be easily dismissed, as he repeatedly cautioned against scepticism and was widely respected in psychic circles as a diligent observer and a man who prided himself on keeping accurate records.

In a private letter to parapsychologist Guy Playfair in 1976, Dingwall stated his views: 'We know practically nothing about the "real" nature of the material world in which we live... the more we peer into our surroundings the most indefinite becomes the boundary. The investigation of the relationship between matter and what you call spirit is only just beginning.... The scrapheap of science is high with discarded theories derived from insufficient experimentation.'

Real or Fake?

There are arguably more fake spirit photographs and phantom film clips now than at any time since the phenomenon came to light, because such images are so easy to create today. Almost every schoolchild knows how to use a computer to manipulate images and edit video. However, among the obvious hoaxes there are occasional images that defy rational explanation.

The much-published shot of the 'uninvited guest' at a holidaymaker's farewell party in 1988 is one such example. In this picture, a group of guests are seated round a table at the Hotel Vier Jahreszeiten in Maurach, Austria. To take the photo, a camera was set up on an adjacent table and the timer was primed, but when the shutter clicked the flash failed to trigger. A second shot was set up and this time the flash fired. When the prints came back from the laboratory the group discovered they had a new member – the head of a young woman can clearly be seen materializing at the edge of the table. Her head is noticeably larger than those of the other guests and she is slightly out of focus. This would suggest that her image comes from a previous undeveloped shot, making the photograph an accidental double exposure – yet neither the photographer nor anyone else at the party recognized the woman. The Royal Photographic Society and the photographic department at Leicester

University subjected both the print and negative to rigorous tests and concluded that it was not a case of double exposure.

The 'Guildhall Monk' is another example. In January 1985, St Mary's Guildhall was the setting for a formal dinner hosted by the Coventry Freemen's Guild. As the guests bowed their heads in prayer, a photograph was taken. When it was developed, the group of guests had been joined by a tall, hooded figure in what looked like a monk's habit. The mayor affirmed that no one had attended the dinner dressed in that fashion, and none of the other guests recalled seeing a person in such clothes. It is worth noting that the building dates from the 14th century and served as a prison for Mary, Queen of Scots.

THE PHANTOM PILOT AND THE WOMAN IN WHITE

The 'Phantom Pilot' is another case that appears to substantiate belief in ghosts. In 1987, Mrs Sayer and a group of friends were visiting the Fleet Air Arm Station at Yelverton in southwest England. Mrs Sayer was persuaded to sit in the cockpit of a helicopter and have her picture taken. She remembers it was a hot summer's day, yet she felt cold sitting in the co-pilot's seat. Of the number of snaps taken, only one came out and it showed a hazy figure in a white shirt sitting in the pilot's seat next to Mrs Sayer. The helicopter had seen action in the Falklands War, but it is not known whether or not the pilot had been killed.

The 'Woman in White' is another convincing example. On 10 August 1991, Mari Huff, a member of the Ghost Research Society, took a photograph at Bachelor's Grove Cemetery near Chicago. The cemetery was noted for occurrences such as strange lights, unearthly sounds and sightings of hooded figures, so the GRS brought cameras loaded with high-speed infrared black-and-white film that was acutely sensitive to low light sources. The GRS saw nothing extraordinary until Mari's film was developed. Her photo clearly shows a young woman dressed in white, sitting on a tombstone. She appears to be brooding and her dress is old-fashioned and semi-transparent. It looks like a 'classic' ghost photo of the kind that might adorn a book jacket, but Mari and her colleagues swear that this is what the camera 'saw' that day.

With the advent of digital photography and image manipulation software, one might think that spirit photography is an anachronism from a more innocent age. But photographs purporting to show glowing orbs, blurred shadowy figures and milky-white phantoms

47

continue to appear in periodicals and on the internet. The fact that some of these images have been subjected to analysis by sophisticated software and declared 'genuine' (or at least 'un-tampered with') only intensifies our enduring fascination with paranormal phenomena. We all know how such effects are created and how easily we can be deceived, but it seems we still need to believe in the paranormal because we live in hope of a better life – for many of us, the life that begins after our present one ends.

SIMULACRA

A final word of caution, before you are tempted to see ghostly faces and figures in your own family photographs. The human brain is wired to identify patterns so that we can recognize familiar faces and distinguish friend from foe. The problem is that we often 'see' faces where there are none. An example of this is the famous 'Face on Mars', which prompted wild speculation among purveyors of the 'ancient astronaut' theory that there was now irrefutable evidence of the remains of pyramid-like structures on the planet's surface. It was later revealed to be nothing more than a play of shadows. This is such a common phenomenon that scientists have given it a name, matrixing (or pareidolia), and the illusory objects it produces are known as simulacra.

SIMULACRA

One of the most macabre examples of a simulacrum is that of the 'Tennessee Electric Chair'. When the state penitentiary decided that 'Old Sparky' needed modifying, the job was given to local engineer Fred Leuchter who had it delivered to his basement workshop. The chair had been made of timber from the local gallows, so it had violently despatched more than its share of miscreants and no doubt some poor innocent souls too, making it a prime candidate for a haunting. Leuchter took several photographs before he began his work. In some of these there are luminous orbs, which could be reflections; but something that appears to be a human hand grips an armrest on the chair, although it has been suggested that this, too, is a reflection. One image in particular invites a second look – that of a face at the back of the chair. The strangest aspect is the size of the face, which is much smaller than a human head would be if a living person occupied the chair. Remember, in the Austrian party photograph described on page 45, the disembodied head of the 'uninvited guest' was notably larger than those of the other people seated round the table. If the Austrian image was genuine, then the Tennessee picture might be as well. But it is yet another anomaly that stretches our credulity to the limit.

MOVING IMAGES

If just one of the numerous unexplained photographs is genuine, then it follows that we should be able to capture moving images of a phantom. While it is not unreasonable to assume that the majority of clips posted by private individuals on YouTube and other internet sites are crude hoaxes, the same cannot be said about those sourced from surveillance cameras in public places – particularly if that public place is reputed to be haunted.

In December 2003, security cameras at Hampton Court Palace, a London residence of the Tudor king, Henry VIII, recorded an unidentified male figure opening fire doors that the staff had been given strict instructions to keep shut. The man was robed and had an unnaturally white face; no features were discernible when the frames were frozen or enlarged. One of the palace security guards admitted that his co-workers had been spooked because the face 'didn't look human'. Naturally the press suspected it was a publicity prank, but a spokeswoman for Hampton Court Palace fended off the accusation by assuring journalists that staff were just as baffled as everyone else who had seen the footage. 'My first reaction was that someone was having a laugh, so I asked my colleagues to take a look. We spoke to our costumed guides, but they don't own a costume like that worn by the figure. It is actually quite unnerving.'

Ghost hunters were in no doubt that the cameras had caught a genuine manifestation. The palace is reputedly haunted by several spirits. Jane Seymour, Henry's third wife, died there in childbirth and Catherine Howard, Henry's fifth wife, was imprisoned there before her execution at the Tower of London. Their spirits have been seen on numerous occasions, as has that of Sibell Penn, nursemaid to Seymour's son, Edward. Sibell died in 1562 but was disinterred in 1829, after which a strange sound like that of a spinning wheel was heard and traced to a room she had used for spinning.

An image from the 'fire door' sequence was published to much fanfare in periodicals around the world, but not everyone was convinced. Debunkers make the point that the 'spirit' appears unusually solid and seems strangely familiar with the procedure of securing a modern fire door (the safety handle has to be pulled down and the left-hand door must be closed before the right-hand door)! This makes it more likely that one of the guides in period costume was playing a prank. However, to date no one has admitted responsibility for the Hampton Court 'haunting'.

A RACING CERT

Across the Atlantic in California, a group of paranormal investigators recently recorded a man-sized shadow walking through the bar and exiting through a solid wall at the Del Mar racetrack, a noted haunt of Hollywood celebrities in the 1930s and 1940s. Stars such as Bing Crosby, Mickey Rooney, W. C. Fields and Lucille Ball lived the high life in a private dining club at the track, but the most domineering personality of the era was horse trainer Charlie Whittingham, whose framed photographs still adorn the walls. Numerous witnesses have heard his voice ordering his favourite drink, a martini, and answering their question 'Is anyone there?' with a hearty, disembodied laugh. But his most unnerving appearance was on a night in July 2010, when his shadow was recorded on the paranormal investigators' videotape. As his ghost passes through the wall there is a small flash of light, even though there is nothing but a hall beyond.

Employees have spoken of sensing a cold spot they can measure with their hands when they are feeling brave enough. Some have also seen a small glowing ball floating through the hallways, which then visits each of the guest bedrooms in turn as if searching for something or someone. One or two people have even challenged the celebrity spirits to make their presence known and have been answered with a hoarse laugh or called by name, only to find that they are alone in the room.

THE SCHOOL SPOOK

On 8 August 2008, surveillance cameras recorded what appeared to be the ghost of a child in Asheville High School, North Carolina, which was closed for the summer vacation. The apparition appears as a shadow on the right of the picture by the elevator, then takes form as it reaches the other side. Even the city schools' spokesman Charlie Glazener, who stated he wasn't a believer in ghosts, told local TV reporters that he didn't have an answer and was now 'one step closer to believing in what we don't normally see'. But one has to ask why a child – dead or otherwise – would choose to go to school when he or she didn't have to, and at 3 o'clock in the morning!

GHOSTS OF GETTYSBURG

If you plan to film ghosts but don't live near a castle or haunted house, a battlefield is the next best thing and should be a site worth staking out. Gettysburg, the scene of one of the bloodiest encounters in the American Civil War, has had its share of sightings. In November 2001, a local family saw some lights moving among the trees and decided to investigate. Fortunately, they took a video camera and filmed what they saw. If you are a disbeliever, the short clip won't be enough to convince you, but if you do believe in ghosts, it could freak you out! After a couple of small lights are seen for a second or two, a number of white figures can be glimpsed among the trees in an area of sacred ground that is strictly off-limits to tourists.

OPEN TO DOUBT

It's hard to raise much enthusiasm for a brief clip shot by After Dark Paranormal Investigations, an American organization who set up a camera in an unnamed cemetery and recorded an unusually frisky sprite gambolling in the top right of the frame. While it's possible that a young, prematurely deceased individual might have decided to return from the dead to dance among the tombstones, it's too fleeting an appearance and not sufficiently distinct to be convincing.

Kathy Henley, an employee at Puckett's Car Wrecking Service in Oklahoma City, is convinced that her workplace is haunted by a victim of a fatal crash. In surveillance footage, a white figure can be seen circling the lot as if searching for a car. The three vehicles it approaches were all impounded following fatal accidents and Kathy insists that no one could have climbed the security fence and entered the lot without triggering the alarm. But there is a fair chance that another employee was playing a prank on her, so this sighting will have to be filed as 'doubtful'.

If ghosts are insubstantial vaporous mists of residual energy, it would be possible for them to reflect sufficient light to leave an impression on film. However, there are so few credible examples that, while the evidence for belief in the existence of ghosts may be overwhelming, their appearances on film are woefully insufficient to support it.

2
TALES OF
RESTLESS
SPIRITS

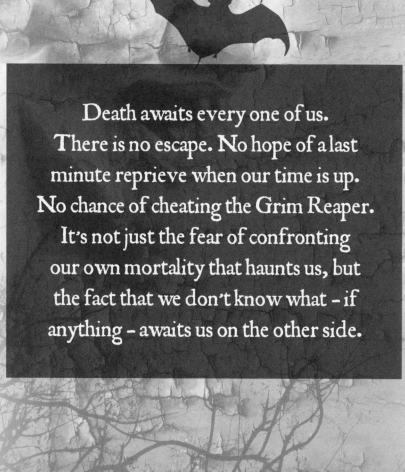

Death awaits every one of us.
There is no escape. No hope of a last
minute reprieve when our time is up.
No chance of cheating the Grim Reaper.
It's not just the fear of confronting
our own mortality that haunts us, but
the fact that we don't know what – if
anything – awaits us on the other side.

Yet we choose to sit in the dark in a movie theatre or in front of our television and get a frisson from films that force us to face the one fear worse than death – that of being tormented by restless spirits who won't sleep soundly in their graves.

From the earliest days of cinema, when the novelty of moving pictures exerted a fascination upon rapt crowds in fairground tent shows and penny arcades, filmmakers have teased us with disturbing images of the unquiet dead. The more gruesome-looking the ghoul, it seems, the better we like it.

Initially, films with supernatural and paranormal themes could be said to reflect the culture of the country that produced them. Classic British shockers such as *Dead of Night* (1945) created an atmosphere of increasing dread in keeping with the fireside ghost stories of M.R. James and Charles Dickens; meanwhile, Hollywood preferred the more lurid horrors of Edgar Allan Poe and Ambrose Bierce, where premature burial and insanity were key elements. British ghosts were often portrayed as fleeting shadows that left much to the viewer's imagination (and were all the more unsettling for that), while Hollywood filmmakers generally believed audiences would feel cheated if they didn't see the evil entity manifest in all its gory glory.

THE POWER OF SUGGESTION

The malevolent presence haunting the owners of a Cornish house in the American supernatural thriller *The Uninvited* (1944) was a rare exception, although the critics who praised the film for not showing the ghost were unaware that it was the British censor who had deleted the scenes showing ectoplasmic apparitions. Another film that restricted its paranormal activity to loud apports, billowing curtains and a 'breathing' door was the original version of *The Haunting* (1963), directed by Robert Wise, who had learnt the power of suggestion from working as assistant to B-movie director Jacques Tourneur in the 1940s. (*The Haunting* was based on Richard Matheson's novel *The Legend of Hell House*, which the author went on to direct under the original title in 1973.)

The low-budget independent production *Carnival of Souls* (1962) took a very different approach, presenting the world of the dead as co-existing with our own.

The film opens with the female lead drowning during a drag race only to find herself 'living' a new life in a dream-like state, unable to interact with the other characters, who may or may not be alive. The awkward, stilted performances of the largely amateur cast are compensated for by visually striking sets, including a derelict amusement park and a gloomy ballroom, which add to the nightmarish quality and have attracted a cult following for the film.

Until the late 1960s, the major movie studios seemed reluctant to feature ghosts in their prestige pictures for fear of alienating members of the audience who might not believe in spirits or for whom a straight horror movie was not to their liking. For this reason, the apparitions who haunt the children in *The Innocents* (1961) are presented as hallucinations conjured up by their prim, sexually repressed governess (Deborah Kerr). The movie is based on *The Turn of the Screw*, a novella by Henry James, and its representation of ghosts runs contrary to the intention of the original author. But whatever interpretation one favours, it does not diminish the shock of Kerr's sighting of a dead woman standing grim-faced by a lake, or the spirit of the dead woman's lover appearing unexpectedly at a window.

VENGEANCE

The same quiet, unsettling atmosphere pervades early Japanese horror movies. The Japanese have a long tradition of supernatural stories, but it wasn't until 1959 that the first memorable entry in the Asian horror canon was released. *Tokaido Yotsuya Kaidan* (*The Ghost of Yotsuya*) is typical in that the vengeful spirits are seen only by the guilty characters, who are tormented by the apparitions until they confess to their crimes or suffer a fitting death, suggesting that these spirits are projections of the criminals' subconscious.

Five years later, Japanese cinema made a striking impression at the Cannes Film Festival thanks to two impressive entries, *Kwaidan* (*Ghost Stories*) and *Onibaba*. The first of these was a portmanteau of traditional ghost stories, somewhat slow and predictable (in one episode a returning samurai spends the night with his wife, only to find himself embraced by her corpse), but highly regarded for its striking use of colour and theatrical effects, including a stylized sea battle and a sequence in which a phantom army of soldiers emerge from their tombs. *Onibaba* is more horror than ghost story, but it features one of the most eerily beautiful images in cinema – that of a dead samurai in a white horned mask which the elderly female protagonist rips off his putrefied face and wears to frighten her daughter.

When she can't remove the mask, the daughter shatters it with a hammer, revealing that her mother is now hideously disfigured too. A sequel of sorts, *Kuroneko* (1968), features the same female characters who, after being murdered by marauding samurai, return from the dead to take their revenge.

While British Hammer Film Productions and their US equivalent, American International Pictures, were resurrecting gothic horror during the 1960s, the Japanese were offering subtler fare based on their own legends and morality tales. *Kaidan Botan Doro* (1968) was lumbered with the crude title *My Bride Is a Ghost* by its American distributor; although a reasonable summary of the plot, the US name for the film doesn't convey the macabre beauty of its imagery or its unsettling effect. The climax of the film is a night scene that takes place during a festival of the dead, when the villagers stand vigil outside the bride and bridegroom's house, banging drums for the souls of their ancestors, before lighting candles which they set afloat on the river. *Kaidan: Yuki Joro* (*Ghost of the Snow Fairy*) (1968) is another stylish supernatural tale based on the same popular legend that inspired a sequence in *Kwaidan*.

Yokai Hyaku Monogatari (*100 Monsters*) (1968) is a Japanese adaptation of *One Thousand and One Nights* and features a collection of ghost stories told to entertain prostitutes and their clients at a newly opened brothel. Unfortunately, the stories are so enthralling that the owner forgets to perform a rite of exorcism and the ghosts materialize to cause havoc in the brothel. Completists might care to check out *Kaidan Kasane-ga-fuchi* (*The Depths*) released in 1957, His *Nou Ai Lueh* (*Four Moods*) from 1970, *Cu'un Sae Han Nyo* (*The Revengeful Ghost*), an atmospheric Korean chiller from 1972, *Gu Jing You Hun* (*Ghost in the Mirror*) from Hong Kong/Taiwan (1974) and *Samwonnyo* (*Valley of Ghosts*) from 1981.

POLTERGEISTS AND POSSESSIONS

During the 1970s, films such as *The Exorcist* (1973) and *The Amityville Horror* (1979) showed there was a global audience for genres beyond the traditional horror movie. US movie producers came to realize that there was profit to be made from dramatizing reputedly 'true' cases of poltergeists and possessions. As if to illustrate this pivotal moment, the schizophrenic Stephen Spielberg/Tobe Hooper collaboration *Poltergeist* (1982) combined Spielberg's sentimental suburban-family-under-threat story with Hooper-inspired scenes of graphic horror.

The ghosts who inhabit the vacant rooms of the remote

snowbound Overlook Hotel in Stanley Kubrick's *The Shining* (1980), after the book by Stephen King, provide some of the more traumatic images in the film, but they are peripheral to the plot, which is primarily concerned with the central character's descent into madness. The twin sisters who appear mute and motionless in a corridor are given a brief back-story, but the cadaverous old woman in the bath-tub and the businessman and his fat friend in the furry animal costume are left mysteriously unexplained and get under the skin and trouble us long after the credits have rolled. The reason for their lingering presence is left to our imagination (in marked contrast to the cliché-ridden gross-out shocker *Ghost Story*, starring Fred Astaire and three fellow Hollywood veterans, released the following year). This unexplained and unresolved element is also a feature of many Asian horror movies, which deliberately play against traditional ghost story conventions. The air of repressed emotion makes such films captivatingly bleak and disconcerting.

SPANISH SPOOKS

The seminal Spanish horror film *Sobrenatural* (*Supernatural*) was released in 1982. It, too, emphasizes atmosphere over action, as a young widow struggles to retain her sanity while being haunted by the spirit of her pathologically dominant husband. At first she refuses to believe he is the cause of the violent disturbances that plague her home, despite all evidence to the contrary, but with the aid of a psychic and a priest she finally accepts he is to blame and manages to exorcise his presence from the house.

The Spanish have contributed a number of impressive horror films in recent years, including the critically and commercially successful *The Devil's Backbone* (2001) and *The Orphanage* (2007). These examples of intelligent, multi-layered movie-making combine a compelling story, an atmospheric setting and well-developed characters. The movies challenge the expectations of a conventional horror movie audience and manage to appeal both to the international art-house crowd and mainstream cinemagoers.

Nevertheless, it was Asian cinema that dominated the horror market in the years around the new millennium, although few Asian movies were traditional ghost stories. *Whispering Corridors* (1998), from Korea, intersperses creaking doors and empty classrooms with short sharp shocks of graphic violence, as a dead schoolgirl takes revenge on her tormentors. *The Ring* trilogy centres on a cursed videotape and its effects on those who watch it, while *The Grudge* series (*Ju-On*, to give it its original title) is a haunted-house chiller with a fractured narrative that adds considerably to its unsettling effect. Both series were remade with bigger budgets and star names (Sarah Michelle Gellar and Naomi Watts) by Hollywood studios who evidently knew a profitable franchise when they saw one. Although low on gore and violence, the remakes capture the brooding creepiness of the originals, which portrayed the malevolent spirits as residual images recorded in the material of accursed objects or in the fabric of a building where a tragedy has taken place. These movies revitalized the supernatural horror genre and gave a younger generation of filmmakers new tricks and techniques with which to jolt the predominantly teenage audience out of their cynicism. From now on, cinema audiences wouldn't accept ghosts as amorphous vapours or pale-skinned cadavers rising from their tombs; instead they would demand that spooks twitch and shudder like distressed digital creations caught between dimensions. For this reason, the big-budget remake of *The Haunting* (1999), starring Liam Neeson and Catherine Zeta-Jones, flopped at the box office even though it was sumptuous to look at (the misty apparitions were not sufficiently terrifying for modern audiences). In contrast, the low-budget remakes of showman William Castle's 1960s' exploitation movies *The House on Haunted Hill* (1999) and *Thir13en Ghosts* (2001) turned a healthy profit because the ghosts were designed to appeal to the gross-out gamer generation.

THE THINKING PERSON'S HORROR FILM

The major American studios didn't neglect the horror genre during this period. Maverick writer-director M. Night Shyamalan takes the credit for creating that rarest of gems, the thinking person's horror film. In *The Sixth Sense* (1999), action man Bruce Willis plays against type as a troubled psychologist who agrees to help a young boy (Haley Joel Osment) who claims he can see dead people. The double-edged 'gift' of clairvoyance is treated seriously and truthfully and gives a reasonable impression of what mediums experience and how they communicate with the dead. *Stir of Echoes* (1999) tried much the same approach and features Kevin Bacon tormented by visions of the ghost of a murder victim who won't rest in peace. Similarly, in *The Gift* (2000), small-town psychic Cate Blanchett solves a murder by communing with the spirit of the victim. In *What Lies Beneath* (2000), Michelle Pfeiffer discovers her latent clairvoyant powers in order to uncover skeletons in her family closet. This underrated supernatural thriller, co-starring Harrison Ford and made in the Hitchcockian manner, had little impact on its release, but it succeeds in being both hugely entertaining and realistic, proving that Hollywood can produce grown-up ghost stories when it has the will and the right material. It did so again with *The Others* (2001) although, like *The Sixth Sense*, this film was directed by an outsider – the Chilean-Spanish director Alejandro Amenábar. *The Others* inverts the traditional haunted house drama to deliver an unexpected twist; by downplaying the supernatural element, it makes the single shock-cut all the more frightening. The unrelated but equally literate *The Awakening* (2011) can be considered a companion piece as the two films share the same contemplative quality and theme – namely that a ghost is not a cadaverous ghoul, but a lost soul in limbo. This film also boasts a shock revelation and is shrewd in the manner in which it encourages the viewer to identify with the sceptical female investigator by having her expose a fake medium in the opening sequence. As evidence for the existence of ghosts mounts up in subsequent scenes, her scepticism dissolves, and the audience, too, is confronted with the realization that ghosts are not the amorphous phantoms we had imagined.

A production of the period drama *The Woman in Black* (2012), devised as a starring vehicle for Daniel Radcliffe, appeared to renew interest in the gothic ghost story, but it seems unlikely to prompt a series of such films. The audience for period pictures has no great appetite for supernatural themes, but will make an exception for a 'classic' chiller. At the same time, horror movie producers in general are not ashamed to admit that they need an undiscerning audience with a considerable disposable income, who can be persuaded to buy a cinema ticket or rent a DVD on the strength of the poster and title alone.

Ghosts can now be seen and heard on computer screens – see *Kairo* (2001) and its US remake *Pulse* (2006) – via mobile phones (*Phone*, 2002), in digital photographs (*Shutter*, 2008), through electronic voice phenomena (*White Noise*, 2005), and even by way of musical instruments (*Cello*, 2005), baby monitors (*The Baby's Room*, 2006) and mirrors (*Mirrors*, 2008). It was perhaps inevitable that eventually a paranormal reality television series would become the basis for a fictional horror movie (*Grave Encounters*, 2011), as would a ghost-hunting investigation (*The Innkeepers*, 2011) and a lab experiment (*The Apparition*, 2012). The latter throws every proven ingredient into the mix (*Blair-Witch-Project*-style camcorder footage, a fear-generated virus – from *The Tingler* – poltergeist activity and bodies on the ceiling from just about every horror genre film of the past two decades) in the hope that something interesting will result. Which begs the question – what variations on the hoary old ghost story are left for filmmakers to explore? And, more significantly, will the increasing popularity of these films encourage viewers to explore the paranormal for themselves?

TELEVISUAL GHOSTS

In 1992, the BBC broadcast a fake paranormal reality programme that caused alarm throughout Britain – equivalent to the panic generated by Orson Welles' notorious 'War of the Worlds' fake newscast on American radio in the 1930s. The programme, *Ghost Watch*, was also significant because it marked the start of the modern paranormal reality shows that are now a staple of the television schedules.

The first sign that something nasty was about to invade our living rooms came in the 1970s, when the success of the movie *The Exorcist* prompted TV producers to consider how they might replicate its shock appeal on the small screen. Obviously, a fictional horror story would not carry the same visceral thrill as something presented as real (one reason for the appeal of *The Exorcist* was that it claimed to be based on a true story). So someone at the BBC had the bright idea of transposing elements of *The Exorcist* from Georgetown, Washington, to suburban London. If the viewing public could be persuaded that evil entities could take over a modest house in Middlesex, the ratings would go through the roof. And who better to put forward such a notion than 'Auntie', as the BBC was affectionately known, home to *The Two Ronnies*, *Blue Peter*, *Nationwide* and other comfortable family teatime entertainment. 'Auntie' never lied – so if the corporation put its name to a documentary programme it must be real, surely?

At first, reporters were content to interview the residents of a supposedly haunted house. They would film the local vicar, accompanied by an exorcist sprinkling holy water on the furniture and reciting the Latin text of exorcism, but this quickly became repetitive. A new approach was needed to keep the viewers' attention. Enter the psychic, to bring a sense of melodrama and mystery.

One of the first experts to attain fame was Maurice Grosse, an investigator for the Society of Psychical Research. Grosse was brought in by the *Nationwide* programme to investigate the alleged haunting of a modest semi-detached house in Enfield, Middlesex, where Mrs Peggy Hodgson and her four children were being tormented by loud bangs and objects that seemed to have a life of their own. As documentary film-maker Adam Curtis observed in his excellent survey of the phenomenon, 'Ghosts in the Living Room' (on the

BBC website), the arrival of the TV crew and their quiet, objective documentary approach turned a novelty news item into 'an intense psychodrama'. In this story, ordinary household items took on a sometimes sinister significance and the children of the house were no longer depicted as helpless victims, but possibly complicit in the deception. (The children later admitted to creating some extra 'effects' to keep the TV crew interested.)

SLIDING CHAIRS AND FLYING LEGO

But even if the children were responsible for some of the strange happenings, they could not have carried out all of them. One of the most unnerving incidents was witnessed by two police officers called to the scene by a neighbour from the adjoining house. The neighbour, Vic Nottingham, had heard a series of raps on the wall but, after being invited into the Hodgson house to investigate, could find nothing to explain them. According to a statement made by one of the officers, while he and his colleague waited in the living room in anticipation of another series of noises they saw a chair slide several feet across the floor by itself. The officer checked the chair, but could find nothing to explain how it had moved unaided. Mr Nottingham recalled that the police had seemed as anxious as he was to leave! Nevertheless, he returned the next night in the hope of solving the mystery, only to be attacked by pieces of Lego which flew out from a box under the bed and hit him hard enough to 'raise a lump' on his elbow.

With the police refusing to become involved as no law had been broken, and with Mrs Hodgson's health suffering as a result of the stress, it was time to call in specialist Maurice Grosse. The era of the small-screen paranormal investigator had begun. From that moment on, the alleged poltergeist activity was recorded on tape, as were the reactions of the children and Grosse's commentary detailing what he witnessed. Four times, a bedside lamp was pulled out of its socket and thrown across the room. Then, after a brief respite, the bedroom door began to shake. When Grosse went to investigate, a plimsoll was hurled across the room and struck the door (though the odds are that one of the children produced that particular effect). Grosse and various family members also witnessed a small sofa rise 30 cm (12 in) in the air; it was then upturned and thrown down again as if by invisible hands – not a stunt that kids could have done without at least one of the adults knowing about it. However, none of this was recorded on camera, so we only have the testimony of the people who were present at the time.

The Poltergeist Solution

Poltergeist activity is commonly attributed to malevolent spirits (the word derives from the German term for 'noisy ghosts') or spontaneous psychokinesis (mind over matter). But a third possible explanation (which doesn't exclude the other two theories

as the source of certain phenomena) was recently advanced by Canadian scientist John Hutchinson who discovered, by accident, that electromagnetic equipment is capable of producing pools of water, moving objects, bending metal, projecting small objects across a short distance and causing other physical phenomena that have traditionally been attributed to poltergeists.

INTERVIEW WITH A POLTERGEIST

Less convincing was the 'interview' Grosse claimed to have had with the spirit, during which his questions were answered by one knock for 'no' and two knocks for 'yes'. As it was conducted in the dark, it would have been easy for one of the children to have rapped on the wall in response, but there was no easy explanation for the appearance of a pool of water on the kitchen floor in broad daylight (see the box on this page for a possible explanation). This was witnessed by Mrs Nottingham, who had nothing to be gained from conspiring with the Hodgson children (if, indeed, they were concocting an elaborate game). On that same occasion, their neighbour also witnessed the kitchen table tipping up of its own accord, doors opening when there was no one in the room and the downstairs toilet flushing by itself. It is claimed that the toilet door had opened and the lavatory brush had risen out of its container to lie flat on the seat – all while the room was empty. Mr Nottingham also told the reporter he had seen a leather chair fly across the bedroom.

Whatever qualities Grosse might have possessed as an amateur ghost-hunter, they were not matched by his ability to deal with the 'ghost'. It stubbornly refused to obey his pleas to leave the family in peace (assuming that 'one rap for no' was an accurate interpretation of its response to Grosse's request for it to desist). Grosse was left to state on camera that the Enfield poltergeist could be one of the most convincing examples on record. But he seemed far too trusting, if not downright gullible, in accepting all the incidents as genuine, especially where the more obvious antics of the two daughters, Margaret and Janet, were concerned. Janet's all-too-obvious attempts to produce a demonic 'voice' would not have fooled an amateur ventriloquist! But what the viewers did not know at the time was that Grosse had recently lost his 22-year-old daughter in a traffic accident. This tragedy had spurred him to seek proof of life after death. It had made him sensitive and compassionate, but perhaps not the most objective of investigators.

The Enfield case became a national talking point, prompting many similar reports and ensuring that Maurice Grosse became a household name. But it soon became apparent that there was little entertainment value to be gained from the sight of a person describing phenomena which only he or she had experienced, or watching objects being thrown by a camera assistant in a 'dramatic reconstruction' of alleged events. What was needed was a more immediate and engaging format that promised to show paranormal phenomena 'live', as they happened.

DRAMA SERIES

TV writer Stephen Volk pitched an idea for a drama series based on the Enfield poltergeist and the multitude of shows that had followed it. The series would shadow a psychic and a TV reporter as they investigated a fictional suburban haunting and it would climax with an episode in which the malevolent spirits finally manifested and trashed the house. Volk's producer suggested that it would be even better if they skipped the atmospheric preamble and went straight to the mayhem. The result would be a one-hour drama that would get viewers (and the press) talking about how TV influences people's behaviour and beliefs. The use of the docudrama and dramadoc formats blurred the distinction between factual reportage and fictional programming. *Ghost Watch* would force the viewer to question what was drama and what was not. As Adam Curtis remarked in 'Ghosts in the Living Room', it had come to a point where no one accepted anything as fact until they had seen it on television, and it was this attitude that *Ghost Watch* was eager to challenge and exploit.

Although the opening titles made it clear that it was a drama, and the timing of the broadcast on Halloween night highlighted that impression, the programme took the form of a fictional live news report. The use of hand-held and infra-red cameras, and a studio set reminiscent of *Crimewatch*, with a bank of monitors relaying feed from various rooms in the fake haunted house, all gave the impression that this was a fly-on-the-wall documentary. The fact that it was co-presented by trusted talk-show host Michael Parkinson, Blue Peter presenter Sarah Greene and Radio 1 DJ Mike Smith only served to mislead unwary viewers into believing that what they were seeing was real.

'What you are about to see is a unique live investigation into the supernatural,' intoned Parkinson, immediately before a pre-recorded video of alleged paranormal activity in the children's bedroom was screened, prefaced with the credit 'University Research Video – 10pm'. Objects were thrown by unseen hands, off-screen rapping could be heard and a bedside lamp fell over, the bulb shattering. At no time were the occupants of the suburban house identified as actors, nor was the studio 'expert' who took calls from 'concerned viewers', each of whom was identified by name on screen as if they were taking part in a genuine phone-in. Even the phone line number hooked up to a genuine BBC call centre. But the whole show was a fabrication and all the participants were actors.

Consequently, the BBC switchboard was jammed with thousands of calls from irate and distressed viewers complaining that they had been traumatized by paranormal phenomena in their living rooms and were now afraid to sleep. Many called in to report that they were hearing strange sounds and experiencing other disturbing phenomena in their homes; the callers asked who they could turn to for help. The following day the press seized on the general panic, prompting the BBC top brass to issue a directive ordering relevant departments to deny all knowledge of the programme. It is said that the *Radio Times* was instructed to bin all readers' letters referring to it and editorial staff were allegedly instructed to spike any stories and omit any reference to *Ghost Watch* in future issues.

SPIRIT OF THE AGE

'There is nothing wrong with your television set. Do not attempt to adjust the picture. We are controlling transmission… You are about to participate in a great adventure. You are about to experience the awe and mystery which reaches from the inner mind to – the outer limits.'

The memorable introduction to the 1960s cult science fiction series *The Outer Limits* could just as easily apply to the many paranormal reality TV shows that scramble for audience attention in the early 21st century. Have they uncovered anything substantial, or are they just groping in the dark to entertain us? Are they of any value, or are they merely exploiting our fear of the unknown and sensationalizing the supernatural?

Ghost Hunters was the first of the current crop of American paranormal reality shows and it is one of the most successful. Its first episode, aired in October 2004,

Above: A photograph taken by William Mumler, around 1872, shows a medium in a trance with the spirit presence of a woman behind him. Mumler's claim to be the first to photograph spirits was disputed by New Jersey photographer W. Campbell, whose image of a child in an 'empty chair' is thought to predate Mumler's photograph by a year. Campbell was not able to replicate the effect, so slipped into obscurity.

Above: After examining a photograph of the Coventry Freeman's Guild dinner, held on 22 January 1985, Lord Mayor Walter Brandish noticed a strange hooded figure at the top table on the left. None of the guests could recall having seen this person there at the time. The 14th-century hall has a spooky reputation, so this visitor was presumed to be a ghost from its medieval past.

Above: A scene from the silent German film *Dr Mabuse, der Spieler* (*Dr Mabuse, the Gambler*), made in 1922, shows a séance in full swing.

Above: In this early 20th-century photograph, the 'ectoplasm' is so obviously cheesecloth it is surprising that anyone could have believed otherwise!

Right: In this photo, taken by William Hope around 1920, a couple are seen leaning against a car with the ghost of their dead son in the driver's seat. Hope used double and even triple exposure techniques to create his photographic ghosts. Although he was unmasked as a fraud in 1922, he continued to practise.

Above: This photo was taken by the vicar of Newby Church in North Yorkshire in the early 1960s. The ghostly presence only showed up when the photo was developed.

Above: The Brown Lady descends the staircase at Raynham Hall, Norfolk.

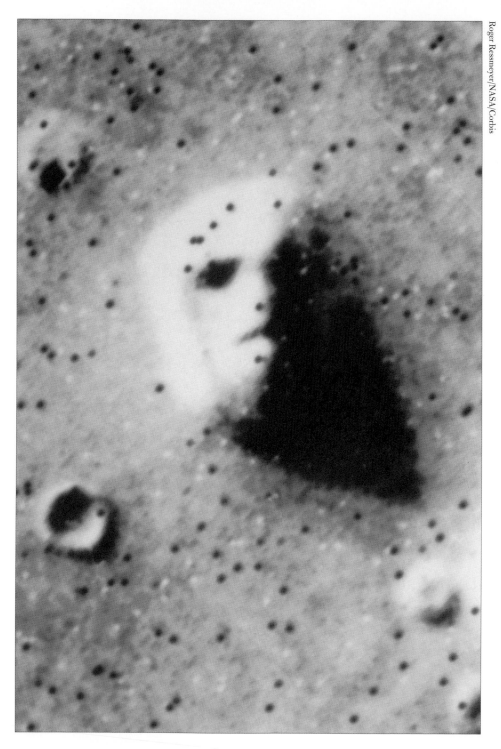

Above: This photograph of the Martian landscape, taken by the Viking space probe in 1976, clearly shows a 'face', but is in fact an illusion known as a simulacrum.

Above: *Poltergeist* (1982), directed by Tobe Hooper, combined family-in-peril suspense with graphic horror.

Above: *The Devil's Backbone* (2001), directed by Guillermo del Toro, is a gothic horror film set during the Spanish Civil War.

Above: Psychic investigator Maurice Grosse with 'souvenirs' of the Enfield poltergeist case.

was based on the format created by the team behind a similarly titled British documentary series which had a brief life on the Discovery Channel in 1996–7. In 2012, the American series was renewed for an eighth season, making it the longest-running reality show on the SyFy Channel (formerly the Sci-Fi Channel).

It gave presenters Grant Wilson and Jason Hawes lucrative new careers and made each of them a household name. It also provided viewers with diverting entertainment. But critics say that after more than a hundred investigations it failed to present any substantial proof of the paranormal, other than a variety of recordings of seemingly random and often inaudible sounds and unexplained strange readings on sophisticated electronic equipment.

Despite being under pressure to produce results, Grant and Jason have admitted that the majority of their investigations failed to produce anything worth transmitting. They say that showing only their successes might have given a false impression of the amount of activity one can expect at a reputedly haunted site. The pair are open and honest about the number of times they have been fooled by cold spots, floating lights and ominous sounds, subsequently discovered to have been draughts, headlights of distant vehicles reflected in a window, moving branches, settling foundations, rats in the walls… all experiences that are an occupational hazard for people paid to grope about in dilapidated buildings at the dead of night.

PARANORMAL STATE

While *Ghost Hunters* is harmless entertainment aimed at promoting idle curiosity in all things paranormal, the first impression one has of *Paranormal State* (2007–) is that it sets out to instil fear and reinforce dangerous preconceptions. This involves asserting that demons and other predatory evil forces not only exist (a highly contentious issue in itself), but are hellbent on taking possession of innocent victims, trashing their homes, playing mischievous mind games and generally making people's lives a misery.

The fundamental flaw of the *Paranormal State* investigations is that there is no attempt at objectivity. The team is made up of devout believers in all things evil and they interpret every sound and symptom as a manifestation of something diabolical. One of the worst examples of this occurred in the exorcism episode 'I Am Six', where a 26-year-old alleged victim is found curled up on the bathroom floor with her mother and other 'witnesses' in attendance. We are shown thin red lines on her skin which the presenter immediately declares to be 'claw marks'! Ignoring the fact that they look suspiciously like scratches made by human fingernails, to make the jump from thin scratches to demonic claw marks is tantamount to saying that all unexplained blemishes on a person's skin are evidence of an alien encounter.

GHOST ADVENTURES

The content of *Ghost Adventures*, which premiered on the Travel Channel in October 2008, is very similar to that of its rivals, only the presenters take a more 'aggressive' approach, taunting the evil entities to show themselves. The one element worth noting is their use of the Ovilus, a controversial electronic device that literally puts words into the mouths of the apparitions (assuming, of course, they are present in the first place). This speech synthesis device was invented by paranormal researcher Bill Chappell. It is marketed 'for entertainment purposes' much like an Ouija board, as the manufacturers can't vouch for claims made by many paranormal groups who use it to 'translate' vibrations from the ether into recognizable speech. The various sensors, which include an EMF meter, apparently combine to generate a number that is converted into phonetic sounds or real words stored in a digital dictionary. This means that if the spirit does not speak English its vibrations can still communicate in the etheric equivalent of Klingon! Not surprisingly, the device has had mixed reviews. There are those who consider it a step forward in inter-world communication, but others think the whole concept is fatally flawed and the words it generates are random and meaningless.

THE HAUNTED

With so many paranormal reality shows vying for ratings it was inevitable that latecomers would have to specialize or offer something different in order to get a look in. *The Haunted* and its spin-off show *Haunted Collector* both offer a novel twist. The former concentrates on hauntings with an animal theme (good-natured pets driven to distraction by a malicious presence in the home) and the latter focuses on artifacts or 'trigger objects' that are believed to be a magnet for malevolent entities.

The team behind *Haunted Collector* undertake pseudo-scientific tests to measure the amount of paranormal activity in the building under investigation. They will, for example, place small objects inside chalk circles to see if they have been moved when no one was in the room. Admittedly, the tests are pretty tame and have little scientific value, but it makes for a more involving show when there is the possibility that the viewer might be treated to the sight of a plastic cow or a large marble moving around all by itself.

The title of *Haunted Collector* refers to self-proclaimed demonologist John Zaffis, who is the leader of this particular team of investigators and curator of his very own paranormal artifacts museum. This houses everything from a religious object allegedly used in occult rituals to mundane items recovered from houses haunted by their previous owners, who couldn't bear to be separated from their possessions after death. Not surprisingly, Zaffis has been criticized for parting vulnerable and gullible people from their possessions on the pretext that they are possessed. But while it is a common belief that objects can be charged with the personal energy of their former owners and that psychics can obtain an impression of that person by holding the object, it seems unlikely that a house could be exorcized simply by removing the object from the property.

GHOST LAB AND THE DEAD FILES

Ghost Lab likes to go where other paranormal investigators fear to tread, but its methods are pretty much the same as its rivals. The *Ghost Lab* crew rolls up in a large trailer packed to the roof with digital monitoring equipment, cameras, audio, EVP meters –

the whole box of tricks – and with a bunch of techies and ghost-hunters who look like they mean business. Meanwhile *The Dead Files* (which premiered in September 2011) keeps it simple and tells it straight, using a genuine medium and teaming her with a hard-bitten detective.

In the third season episode, titled 'Fatal Attachment', *The Dead Files* team is asked to check out a haunted dental surgery in Huntington, West Virginia. Even before she has entered the property, the medium (Amy) gives a fairly detailed description of an elderly man between 6' 2" and 6' 4" in height with steely grey hair. Less than five minutes into the show, she has located the scene of a crime he committed there decades earlier – the murder of his own daughter.

Amy's onscreen partner, Steve DiSchiavi, a former New York City homicide detective, has already spoken to the current tenant, the dentist Dr Grimes, who has kept a detailed log of all the major incidents he, his employees and clients have experienced over the previous couple of years. The doctor's daughter confesses that she too glimpsed the dead girl years ago when she was playing in her father's waiting room. She also said her father had painted an uncannily accurate likeness of the ghost.

RELIVING A DEATH

Amy's intuition leads her to the stairwell, where she describes disturbing vibrations generated by a violent death that make her feel nauseous. Climbing up to the landing, she locates the spot where the girl died, a victim of her father's violent temper. Amy is specific about the injuries and later describes the killer to a sketch artist, who draws a square-jawed older man, a broad-shouldered, outdoor 'cowboy' type, with coarse leathery skin and wavy silver-grey hair. The artist's drawing closely resembles the description of a man who pursued his wife and teenage daughter to the surgery address in 1929 and allegedly murdered the girl in a drunken rage, throwing her down the stairs and causing injuries from which she died ten days later.

The man's name was Sirus Wall and his daughter was called Lavina. A report of the killing in a local newspaper of the time appears to validate Amy's impression that a young girl was murdered by her abusive father. Armed with the newspaper report, a local historian manages to locate a photo of the suspect at the wheel of his truck taken around the time of the murder, so the viewer can appreciate the striking similarity to the drawing made by the sketch artist. Once the two presences have been identified and everyone is aware of who the spirits are, Amy offers a possible 'cure', consisting of substances to be sprinkled or burned inside the building on successive nights to 'cleanse' the air. She recommends a blend of natural herbs for 'blessing and protection', together with holy water and black salt to purify and purge the atmosphere. Apparently Dr Grimes took Amy's advice and managed to clear the intimidating presence of Lavina's father from the building. We are told he continues to commune with the girl in the hope of helping her to move on. So there's a rarity on a paranormal reality show – a happy ending.

THE GHOSTS WHO WEREN'T THERE

Before assuming that every shadow is a restless earthbound spirit and every unexplained incident evidence of paranormal activity, it is worth considering a more mundane theory. The following case was published in the *American Journal of Ophthalmology* in 1921 and is credited to the eminent eye doctor, William Wilmer. Dr Wilmer's patients included eight American presidents and numerous high-profile businessmen, all of whom considered Wilmer a trustworthy man not given to flights of fancy. The story concerns one of his patients, who wished to remain anonymous and who was identified only as Mrs H.

In 1912, Mrs H and her family moved to an old house

that had been empty for ten years. It had no electricity and relied on gas lamps and a furnace for heat and hot water. It was not a cheerful place, but once the servants were installed and going about their chores it was busy with activity. However, within a couple of days both Mrs H and her husband felt depressed and could not account for it. Then the sounds started.

'One morning, I heard footsteps in the room over my head,' Mrs H recalled. 'I hurried up the stairs. To my surprise, the room was empty. I passed into the next room, and then into all the rooms on that floor, and then to the floor above, to find that I was the only person in that part of the house.'

One by one the family members began to complain of listlessness and severe headaches. They lost their appetites and grew pallid and weak. Mr H became irritable and anxious. He said he had sensed a presence standing behind him when his chair faced the fireplace, so he insisted on sitting facing the hall so he could see if anyone entered the room. The children, too, were convinced they were being watched and refused to play in the nursery at the top of the house.

NOISES IN THE NIGHT

A Christmas holiday away from the house restored the spirits of mother and children, but on their return they found Mr H's condition had worsened. He said he had been disturbed by noises at night. Mrs H told Dr Wilmer: 'Several times he was awakened by the sound of a bell ringing, but on going to the front and back doors he could find no one at either. One night he was roused by hearing the fire department dashing up the street and coming to a stop nearby. He hurried to the window and found the street quiet and deserted.'

The servants, too, became increasingly jumpy as they tried to convince one another they had heard sounds and felt an unseen presence. The children succumbed to winter colds, but strangely these improved when they went outside. Then Mrs H was woken in the night by the sound of banging doors, a commotion in the empty kitchen and footsteps ascending a staircase behind her bedroom wall, despite the fact that nothing lay behind the wall. Heavy furniture was heard being moved in the early hours, though everyone was in bed and no one was up and about to move it.

In January 1913, the unseen presences materialized. 'On one occasion,' Mrs H remembered, 'in the middle of the morning, as I passed from the drawing room into the dining room, I was surprised to see at the further end of the drawing room, coming towards me, a strange woman, dark-haired and dressed in black. As I walked steadily on into the dining room to meet her, she disappeared. This happened three different times.'

FROZEN WITH FEAR

On a separate occasion a servant woke to find a young woman and an elderly man sitting on the edge of the bed glowering at her. She froze with fear until what she assumed was a hand tapped her on the shoulder and made her sit up. At this point the apparitions disappeared. Soon after, Mr H was assaulted by an unseen apparition that attempted to strangle him and he began to hear what he assumed were intruders roaming about the house. When he went to investigate, there was no one to be found. By now, the family were at their wits' end. They made enquiries to find out if the previous occupants had experienced something similar and were told that they had – only worse.

'The last occupants we found had exactly the same experiences as ourselves,' Mrs H confided to Dr Wilmer, 'with the exception that some of them had seen visions clad in purple and white crawling around on their beds. Going back still further, we learned that almost everyone had felt ill and had been under a doctor's care, although nothing very definite had been found the matter with them.'

Fortunately, Mr H shared his fears with his brother,

who recalled reading of another family who had suffered from similar incidents many years earlier. The ghostly manifestations, the depression and other disorders, it seemed, were all symptoms of carbon monoxide poisoning.

A physician was summoned, and after he had finished his examination of the family he made a tour of the house. In the basement he made a careful study of the furnace and observed that odourless and tasteless fumes were leaking into the rooms instead of being forced up the chimney. Once the furnace was repaired, the 'ghosts' and their attendant phenomena never returned.

Should you imagine that such cases occurred only in the past, it is worth noting that as recently as 2005 the *American Journal of Emergency Medicine* published an account of a young woman who had fallen unconscious in the shower as a result of carbon monoxide leaking from an improperly installed gas water heater. When she was revived, she told paramedics that just before she passed out she had seen a ghost in the shower!

However, for every discredited case, there are many convincing ones...

KINETIC WOMAN

Many cases of alleged poltergeist activity may be attributed to a natural phenomenon known as psychokinesis. It is thought that teenagers in the throes of emotional and hormonal changes may unconsciously discharge bursts of kinetic energy (as may highly strung or neurotic adults). These spikes of energy can affect electrical appliances and, in extreme cases, move small objects. In one of the best-documented cases of recent times, the disturbances were traced to an intense young woman whose increasing frustration with her monotonous job is thought to have triggered various electrical phenomena.

In November 1967, German solicitor Sigmund Adam received a bill for electricity far in excess of the amount he usually paid to run his small Munich office. This wasn't the only sign that something was wrong. Adam had also been forced to replace burnt-out fluorescent strip lights twice a week, when the lights should have lasted for months. Also, the electricity meter was registering unexplained surges of current which the local electricians could not account for. During tests, their meters registered twice the expected voltage when connected to a 1.5 volt battery. Where was all this energy coming from?

Unable to explain the phenomenon, the power company advised the solicitor to install a generator in case there was a fault in the cables; they also suggested he use bulbs instead of strip lights. But the power surges continued and the bulbs blew as frequently as the fluorescent strip lights. Despite what the electricians told him, Herr Adam assumed it was all down to faulty wiring. Then he received an unusually large telephone bill listing dozens of calls to the speaking clock. Sometimes there were up to six calls a minute, though it was not possible to make that many in so short a time. Just as Herr Adam was thinking of paying the bills and learning to live with the inconvenience and expense, his furniture began moving by itself. A heavy filing cabinet was dragged across the floor by unseen hands and pictures revolved on the walls when no one was near.

By this time, the national newspapers had heard of the case and their reports compelled the Freiberg Institute of Paranormal Research to despatch Professor Hans Bender to investigate. Professor Bender noticed that the disturbances only occurred when 18-year-old office worker Ann-Marie Schaberl was present. Bender was told that the ceiling lights were also seen to swing whenever she walked underneath them and the calls to the speaking clock occurred when she watched the clock intently, praying for the day to end. As soon as Ann-Marie left the office to submit to tests at the Institute, the unusual occurrences ceased.

The tests did not reveal any psychic abilities, though her scores during intuitive and ESP tests increased significantly when she was encouraged to recount her memories of a traumatic illness she had suffered for over a year. It was hoped that talking about this experience might release any pent up fears she still possessed. She returned to work, but the phenomena resumed. Forced to leave her job, she went to work for two other employers and was dismissed by both for the same reason. Then her fiancé ended their engagement, blaming her kinetic 'tantrums' for disrupting the electronic scoring equipment at the bowling alley and ruining their social life! It was only after she met and married another man with whom she had children that the disturbances finally ceased.

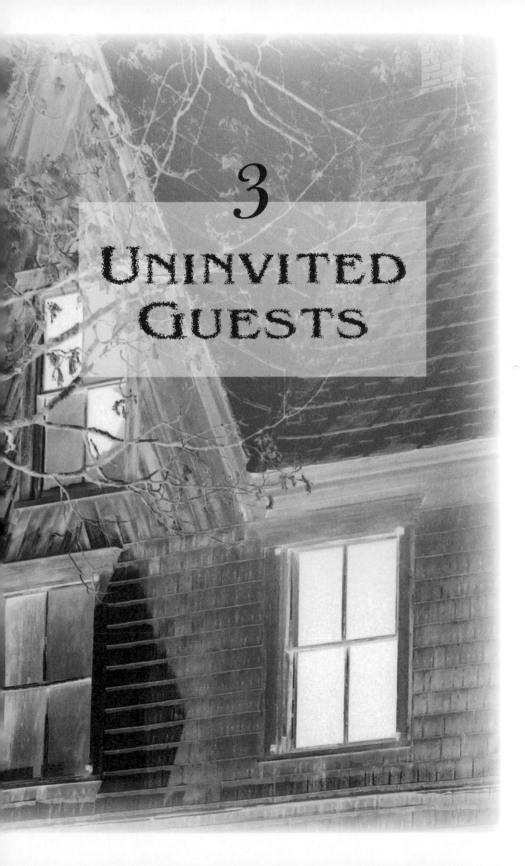

3
UNINVITED GUESTS

There was once a time when any self-respecting ghost would haunt only the grandest of stately homes. But times change, and today even ghosts must settle for what they can get. It's quite a comedown from country house to council house, so perhaps that's why the poltergeists of Prial Avenue in Lincoln, England, are so tetchy.

SPECTRAL SQUATTERS

It seems that Lincoln city council has been inundated with requests from tenants demanding to be relocated to escape spectral squatters who have made their lives a living hell.

Jade Callaby, a 26-year-old single mum, suffered six years of unexplained paranormal activity in her Prial Avenue property. It began with kettles, TVs and toasters switching on by themselves and with objects disappearing from one room only to turn up in another. But then the curious incidents became less playful and more disturbing. Jade and her nine-year-old daughter, Courtney, were startled out of their sleep night after night by loud banging noises. They also claim to have seen shadows when no one else was present in the house.

In desperation Jade called in a priest to 'bless' the house, but the unsettling incidents continued. She was forced to ask the council to relocate her.

'It's been absolutely terrifying,' she told a local reporter. 'Kettles and vacuum cleaners have turned on and off by themselves, cups have moved, dark shadows have appeared and darkened rooms, and my daughter has been woken up by the sound of heavy breathing in front of her face – but nobody was there. I used to try to explain things away, but now I believe – and I'm not staying there another night.'

Lincoln housing official John Morris admitted that Prial Avenue is not the only area of the city to be plagued by ghosts. 'There have been reported cases of haunted council houses in the past, but there has never been any tangible evidence of haunting.' During my research I discovered that, during the Second World War, Prial Avenue and the surrounding streets were decimated by a German air raid in which many residents were killed in their sleep. In the early hours of 8 May 1941, a bomb blew the fronts off four houses, leaving a hole large enough to accommodate two double-decker buses standing one on top of the other. At Westwick Gardens a bomb demolished the back wall of a house, killing a baby and its father. The back garden adjoined Prial Close, where an elderly woman was killed the same night. All these events might account for the hauntings in that area.

THE FORMER TENANT

In March 2000, a paranormal investigation group calling themselves the Ghost Club were invited to a two-bedroom council flat in Woolwich, South London. The tenant, a young mother with a baby daughter, had complained of being tormented by noises, shadows and inexplicable activity. She was so distressed by these disturbances she had told the council that she was willing to move to a smaller flat if necessary.

The hauntings had begun with seemingly insignificant signs, such as her daughter appearing to react to an unseen presence, and the cat running away as if it had been frightened. Then the young woman heard footsteps in an empty room above and a shuffling sound outside her bedroom door, as though someone was pacing restlessly in the hall. She heard the bed creaking as if someone was getting in beside her, and one night the duvet was pulled off. The atmosphere in her daughter's room was often icy and there was a cold draught at the bottom of the stairs. The woman also sensed that someone was watching her from the bottom of the stairs when she walked up to her flat.

There could be a rational reason for all these incidents, but it is harder to explain what happened next. One evening, the young woman walked into her bedroom and saw the shadow of a man in the corner. This shadowy presence had substance and she could see that he was wearing a suit. He was a black man, between thirty and forty years of age, and he appeared to be asleep. He only disappeared after she repeatedly looked away to see if she was imagining the vision. Another night she woke to see a man standing in the corner of the room, before fading away; whether or not it was the same man, she couldn't say.

At this point she became convinced that the house was haunted and decided to contact the previous tenant to see if she had experienced the same feelings. The tenant, who had lived in the flat for eight years, admitted experiencing a constant feeling of being watched. She said she had found her small son talking to an invisible presence he called Peter; the child had also been given to screaming for no apparent reason. His toy car would shoot across the room on its own and the dog would growl unaccountably at the bottom of the stairs. At first, the woman suspected that the presence might be the spirit of her dead father, but then the feelings became so unsettling and unpleasant that she knew it couldn't be him. Other people saw things too: the brother of a friend of hers visited the flat in 1992 and mentioned seeing the shadow of a man in the hallway.

The Ghost Club asked a psychic to check out the

house. He wasn't told any specific details about the sightings or the sounds and he had no prior knowledge of the history of the house, but as soon as he entered he felt he was being watched. He identified the presence as male and traced it to the right-hand corner of the bedroom, where the shadow of the man had been seen. He then entered the child's room and felt that the presence had a connection with a child.

On 6 July, members of the Ghost Club returned with a number of psychics, who picked up on several things they could not have known about in advance. In the bathroom, they sensed that two previous female tenants had suffered miscarriages; this was subsequently confirmed. In the child's room, they picked up on the presence of a man in black, a sense of panic and someone screaming for help.

At 11pm that night, all the visitors to the house heard the sound of footsteps running down the hallway. The group decided to disperse throughout the house and see what impressions they could pick up. One of them had the strong sense that a black man had carried on abusive relationships with the women, one of whom had murdered him. According to one of the psychics, his ghostly presence in the bedroom was because he had lived next door and entered the flat from a balcony that led to the bedroom window.

Following the investigation the female tenant was rehoused and, according to members of the Ghost Club, her personality has undergone a significant change. She is no longer depressed, but happy and relieved to be away from the oppressive atmosphere and out of reach of whatever, or whoever, remains trapped in that house.

THE SHADOW IN THE CELLAR

In May 2001, Steven LaChance, a single father of three living in Union, Missouri, was desperate to find a new home for his family, as the lease on their apartment was about to expire. He had answered many adverts for rental properties, but had found nothing suitable; time was running out. Then he received a phone call from an elderly woman who said she was holding an 'open house' for an old property she wanted to rent. From the moment Steven saw it, he knew it was the perfect home for his family – at least that is what it appeared to be in daylight. It was a white, weather-boarded house with three bedrooms and a basement – plenty of space for a growing family.

Steven's eagerness to move in led him to dismiss the warning signs suggesting that all might not be right with his new home. The first indication that something sinister was lurking in the shadows came when the landlady asked to meet him in a local restaurant to sign the contract and take the deposit. Why, he wondered, hadn't she invited him to the house? Steven noticed she seemed very relieved to get the property off her hands. This struck him as odd because the house was very attractive, with charming original features and was in good condition for its age.

However, from the very first day there were indications all was not well. Pictures fell repeatedly from their hooks even though they had been hung securely, local people crossed the street to avoid walking in front of the house, and neighbours ignored Steven's greetings as though shunning the property and its new inhabitants. The first sign of a malevolent presence came when Steven's youngest son ran screaming from the basement, claiming that something had chased him and that it was 'big'. Steven was alarmed to see a pool of urine at the boy's feet. The child was clearly terrified and nothing his father could say would persuade the child that he had imagined it.

Nothing unusual occurred for a few days, then the family came home to find that all the lights in the house were on even though they had turned them off before going out. There was a noticeable chill in the air in the living room, despite the fact it was midsummer. The next evening, the family discovered what was causing the unexplained disturbances. As they sat watching TV with their backs to the kitchen, a figure appeared in the doorway. The body seemed to form out of a swirling black mist and Steven could hear laboured breathing. Fortunately, the children were glued to the TV, so only Steven saw it. Then the figure vanished. Steven had been planning to take the children to their grandmother's house the next day, but he suddenly felt as though it would be a good idea to leave straightaway! As the children calmly filed out of the house, unaware of why their father had changed his plans, they heard a wail welling up. It was so loud that the neighbour's dogs began to bark. As the family drove away, the youngest son blurted out that the 'basement monster' was watching them from an upstairs window. Steven glanced back to see the same figure he had seen only moments earlier.

A week later, Steven returned from a business trip, collected the children from their grandmother and returned to the house. He told himself that whatever he thought he had seen and experienced was unlikely to recur, but that didn't prevent him from suffering a sleepless night or two.

He called the landlady and tried to sound as casual as he could while probing for information about former tenants. There had been a young woman who moved away suddenly after claiming that her dead father had called on her. She left her belongings in the shed and refused to return to collect them. Another tenant had departed in the middle of the night. He too had abandoned his belongings, which were still in the garden shed.

A MALEVOLENT PRESENCE

That should have been enough to encourage the family to move out, but they hoped that things would quieten down. But it was not to be; the disturbances became more violent and life-threatening. One evening, doors began to bang. Steven assumed his children were the cause, but the younger two were in bed and his daughter was in another part of the house. Then the building began to shake, the temperature dropped and a terrible stench wafted through the rooms. In rising panic, Steven struggled to reach his children, but their bedroom doors were locked. He somehow found the strength to break down the doors and, as he fled into the street with his children, was certain that the malevolent presence was behind them. Once in the car, they drove down the street, then pulled over and looked back. They could see a black shadow moving from room to room upstairs as though it was searching for the occupants.

The children never returned to the house, but Steven had to do so in order to collect their clothes and possessions. But he didn't go alone. On one occasion his brother accompanied him and took a photograph of Steven in the basement. It was an odd thing to do, Steven thought, but maybe his brother wanted something to remind the family of the time they had lived in a haunted house – not that they were ever likely to forget! When the photograph was developed, Steven was not alone in the picture. There, standing behind him, was the shadowy figure of a man dressed in old-fashioned clothes, an angry expression on his face.

The family were more than relieved to have escaped and wanted to forget the whole business, but Steven's brother was curious about the history of the house and its previous inhabitants. He scoured the internet for details and discovered that a Civil War hero, Major General Eugene Asa Carr, had once lived there. The Major's photograph was the spitting image of the malevolent figure who had stood behind Steven in the basement. But the Major had been a hero and there was no mention of what might have caused him, if indeed it was him, to haunt the house. Maybe some spirits simply can't accept that they are dead.

HAUNTED HOTELS

In the 19th century, Virginia City in Nevada was a centre for silver prospectors who had struck it rich and were looking for a wild time. A hundred years later, there was little for tourists to do in the town aside from window shopping, drinking at the many saloons or taking in a show at the Opera House. When Janice Oberding checked into the Silver Queen Hotel after an evening at the theatre, she was ready for a good night's sleep. But in the early hours of the morning she was awoken by a couple arguing in the room next door. The man's voice was raised so loud that Janice could hear it through the wall; she could also hear the woman begging him for forgiveness. Then the man became physically abusive and pushed the woman against the wall. Janice was about to call the desk clerk, but she remembered that in such a small hotel there was unlikely to be anyone on duty at that hour. She would have called the sheriff, but didn't have a cell phone, so she determined to make a complaint in the morning. The verbal abuse and the crying continued and then there was silence. It was now past 3am and Janice was finally able to sleep.

After breakfast Janice reported the row to the manageress, only to be told that the room next to hers was unoccupied. The manageress said the disturbance had been caused by the resident ghosts. Years ago, a man had murdered his girlfriend in that room. If Janice didn't believe it, the manageress said, she would show her. When the two women searched the room they found it empty, but for a decorator's ladder and some paint pots.

At the Balsams Hotel in Dixville Notch, New Hampshire, a female resident woke one morning to see a dripping wet, naked man standing at the foot of her bed. She drowsily assumed it was her husband emerging from the shower; she called out to him, but her husband was sleeping next to her. He woke just in time to corroborate her story. The next instant, the naked figure vanished. It is said that in the 1930s, a band leader who was staying in that room had drowned in a nearby lake.

THE GHOST BOOK

Hotels are required to keep a register of their guests, but one hotel in Bisbee, Arizona, keeps a register of its ghosts too.

The Copper Queen Hotel has a long and eventful history dating back to 1902. Hotel staff are happy to share this colourful past with inquisitive guests, many of whom book in for that very reason. The desk clerk relates how he heard a woman's voice in the elevator when he was the only person in it at the time. If you ask nicely, he will open the ghost register – a record of the activities of the non-paying residents who checked out a hundred years ago. The entries describe many seemingly insignificant but unsettling incidents, such as a child's soft toy playing hide and seek with its owner, and the inexplicable failure of cameras and cell phones in certain 'dead spots'. There have been various sightings of a ghostly boy called Billy who has been seen jumping on a leather couch in the lobby, decades after he was found drowned in a nearby river. Some guests have reported encountering a bearded man in a top hat, who leaves behind a trail of cigar smoke; other male guests claim to have been 'interfered with' by the ghost of a prostitute who is said to have committed suicide in the hotel.

All told, there are said to be sixteen spirits haunting Bisbee, enough to encourage a local historian to organize a ghost tour of the town conducted from the driving seat of a secondhand hearse.

THE MANY GHOSTS OF THE MYRTLES MANSION

The old plantation mansions of the Deep South, particularly those in Louisiana, have a singular atmosphere, shrouded as they are in Spanish moss and veiled in creeping fog seeping in from the bayou. Of all the houses in St Francisville, the Myrtles mansion (built in 1796 for Deputy Attorney General David Bradford) is considered to be one of the most haunted in the United States. However, in their enthusiasm to find wraiths under every bed some ghost-hunters have mistakenly attributed too many spooks to the site, which is now doing a thriving trade as a historic guesthouse.

Nevertheless, several guests have spoken of being approached by slaves and domestic servants who ask what they can do for the guests, before fading in front of their eyes. A gateman quit the guesthouse after welcoming a lady in a white dress, who walked up to the house and promptly disappeared through the (closed) front door! In the evening the piano has been heard to play one melancholy chord over and over again, but no one is seen sitting at the keyboard.

One visitor, Stacey Jones, founder of the Central New York Ghost Hunters group, enthused, 'It is a spectacular place to stay, if you keep an open mind. While taking the guided tour, I saw what looked like a heavyset African-American woman wearing an apron walk by the door, on the porch. Thinking it was a worker in period dress, I peeked out and no one was there.' Stacey's friend, a devout sceptic, apparently had a distressing experience when lying in bed that night. Pinned down by unseen hands, she was unable to move or cry out. Eventually, the unseen presence tired of the game and released her.

FICTITIOUS PHANTOMS

While there is no shortage of spirits on the 240 hectare (600 acre) plantation and some claim that ten murders have been committed there, only one killing has been confirmed.

A former slave named Chloe is said to have been hanged for the murder of three children, whose ghosts have been seen playing on the veranda. Both Chloe and her crimes are now believed to be nothing more than morbid fancies – even though at least one house guest has claimed to have seen her. In the late 1980s, Frances Myers was staying in one of the downstairs rooms when she awoke to find a black woman in a long dress standing beside her bed. The apparition was wearing a green scarf or shawl around her head and holding a candle which emitted a faint glow. Frances screamed and hid under the covers; when she looked again, the ghost was gone. It may be that she saw 'Chloe's Ghost', the spirit whose blurry shadow is seen on one of the postcards sold on the site. But a close look at the photograph reveals the face of a much older woman than the one Frances described.

Children's voices have been heard throughout the house and a little girl with golden ringlets and wearing a Victorian era dress has been sighted peering through the window of the games room. This room was used as a makeshift infirmary during the yellow fever epidemic that claimed several of the former owner's children.

The only murder to have been substantiated is that of

attorney William Winter, who was shot by an unnamed assassin in 1871 as he stood on the side porch. Legend has it that Winter dragged himself to the staircase, where he expired in his wife's arms. Guests and guides claim to have heard his footsteps echoing in the hall as he staggers up the steps; they also say they have heard him give his last dying gasp, but the fact is that William Winter died where he fell. The assassin escaped on horseback and was never brought to trial. Winter's wife died of a broken heart seven years later, aged forty-four.

While legends of the ghostly inhabitants may be greatly exaggerated, the house seems to have been cursed from the moment the first nails were put in.

YELLOW FEVER

The mansion's first owner sold the plantation, which was then known as Laurel Grove, for several hundred barrels of flour. At the time flour was in short supply and he hoped to make a fortune by selling it on, but the flour was never delivered and he died an embittered man. The next owner was distraught with grief when his children succumbed to yellow fever during an epidemic that scoured the region. Unable to remain in the house, he sold it to the wealthy Stirling family, who rebuilt it, doubling its size by adding a southern extension and introducing many imposing features, including a front gallery

32 m (107 ft) long. After furnishing the rooms with European art and antiques, they renamed the estate the Myrtles.

But four years later the master of the house died, leaving the property to his formidable wife, Mary. Four of the couple's children had died young and their eldest son died the same year as his father. It is thought that these may be the spirits who haunt the house to this day, reliving happier times of wealth and privilege. The dark days at the end of the Civil War saw the house and plantation looted by federal troops; after the Confederacy surrendered to the Union in 1865, the family fortune was rendered worthless. Following a succession of owners, the house passed to a family whose son had drowned during a storm.

CHLOE THE SLAVE

In the 1950s the house was sold to a widow, Marjorie Munson, and that is when the ghost stories began. Marjorie was tormented by unexplained occurrences and asked her neighbours if any of them had heard if the house was haunted. There was a local legend of an old woman in a green bonnet, but she had no name; it was only when James and Frances Kermeen purchased the house in the 1970s that the legend of Chloe the slave was born. It was said that Chloe wore the green headband to cover a gaping wound where her ear had been cut off as punishment for eavesdropping. Even more lurid and fanciful was the tale of how the slave had been abused by her master (in truth, a man known to have been uncommonly kind to his servants) and then abandoned. She was said to have sought revenge by poisoning his three children, a crime for which she was hanged by her fellow slaves. In fact, two of the children she was accused of killing died several years apart and the third was not even born at the time of the alleged crime. Exhaustive research by historian David Wiseheart failed to find any record of a slave by the name of Chloe. Other graphic crimes said to have been committed on the plantation were equally without foundation.

BLOOD ON THE FLOORBOARDS

Of the six murder victims named in previous histories of the house, one was found to have died of yellow fever (not stabbed to death over a gambling debt, as local legend would have it); the tale of three Union soldiers who were shot during a looting spree was also exposed as a complete fallacy. In echoes of numerous other ghost stories, it was said that their bloodstains on the floorboards could not be scrubbed clean, but no account of their murder could be found in the local newspapers or military archives. The story of the fifth 'victim', a caretaker killed during an attempted burglary in 1927, may have been inspired by the murder of a local man in another building on the plantation around the same time.

THE HAUNTED MIRROR

Even though many of the ghosts have been dispatched by diligent research, some enthusiasts remain stubbornly devoted to the mansion's reputation and point to the 'haunted mirror' as evidence of its supernatural cachet. Photographs of this antique-looking mirror appear to show a cluster of phantom hands imprinted behind the glass. When this was pointed out to the present owners, they had the glass professionally cleaned, but the prints could not be erased. They replaced the glass and still the prints were seen when the guests had their snapshots developed. The latest theory is that the impressions are flaws in the wood which appear in the shape of handprints when the flashlight catches the indentations.

It would seem that the only certain way to evaluate the paranormal quotient of the Myrtles is to check in and see what happens. Is any one brave enough to check in and take their chances?

IN THE STILL OF THE NIGHT

The Myrtle mansion is an essential stopover for any serious ghost hunter, but there's another haunted plantation house that is off the official tourist map. Legendary country music singer Loretta Lynn was raised a God-fearing Christian in the mountains of Kentucky, but she is not ashamed or afraid of her psychic abilities, which she believes she inherits from her mother. When she was living with her first husband and feeling homesick, she would often sense when a letter from home was about to be delivered and what its contents would be, as though she could read her mother's thoughts while she was writing it. Loretta also experienced several premonitions, including one where she saw her father lying in a casket the day before she heard he had died. Many years later, when she visited her childhood home in Butcher Hollow, she saw his ghost sitting on the front porch.

Then in the late 1960s, after becoming an internationally famous country music star, Loretta was driving though Tennessee, house-hunting with her husband, when they took a wrong turn and came upon a historic plantation house in Hurricane Mills. They were so enamoured with the house that they bought the nearby town as well!

However, shortly after they moved in, strange and

unsettling things occurred. Doors would open and close by themselves, a woman in period clothes would appear in the children's bedroom and the sound of a woman walking up the stairs in high heels could be heard in the still of the night. Loretta believes the sounds were made by a woman in white who she saw standing on the second-floor balcony, wringing her hands and sobbing. She is said to be the ghost of Beula Anderson, the wife of a former owner of the plantation who died days after losing her newborn child. Both mother and child are buried near the house.

The sound of rattling chains has also been heard from the slave pit, a cellar where slaves were confined for disobeying their white owners, and shadows have been seen moving through the upstairs rooms, where cold spots have been felt by believers and non-believers alike. The singer's personal assistant has reported hearing noises when she was staying alone in the house. But not all the house guests are mere shadows. Both Loretta and her granddaughter have been woken several times in the night by a man in black standing at the foot of their bed – and it wasn't Johnny Cash! When Loretta's son Jack went to sleep with his boots on, the spectre of a confederate soldier tried to remove them, as if to say, 'a Southern gentleman is never too drunk or too tired to take his boots off in the house'. The family later learnt that a number of rebel soldiers had been buried on their land after a fire-fight during the Civil War. Sadly, Jack later drowned in the river that runs through the plantation, a tragedy his grandmother had foreseen, but was powerless to prevent.

Despite its tragic past, Loretta has learned to live with the former inhabitants of her home and doesn't mind sharing it with them: 'As long as you're good to ghosts, they'll be good to you. I don't make them mad.'

THE NIGHT VISITOR

When terminally ill or elderly people move into a hospice, they don't expect to leave alive. Perhaps that is why some of them remain within its walls after they die. The Homestead Nursing Home in New Jersey is one such place. It eventually closed and was converted into an apartment block, but those who lived there swore they were visited by the ghosts of former patients.

As a teenager, Markus Misery (his real name) was fascinated rather than frightened when told the history of the building into which his family had just moved. He would explore the crawl spaces in the basement, where he found artifacts including dental records and receipts for food supplies. But nothing untoward happened until, years later, Markus returned home from serving in the army. In bed one night he experienced deep sleep paralysis, a natural phenomenon attributable to extreme fatigue. It is quite common and occurs when a person wakes from a deep sleep to find himself unable to move or cry out because his body has become rigid, even though his mind is alert. This state has given rise to the myth of the 'night hag', who sits astride the sleeper and sucks the breath of life from his body until he struggles to wake and cast her off. It's a form of nightmare, but it seems very real at the time as it is accompanied by pressure on the chest which feels as though something or someone is pinning the sleeper down.

Markus was evidently exhausted after the physical trials of army training, but the 'night hag' experience cannot account for what happened next. On more than one occasion he felt someone climb into bed next to him and, although fear forced him to keep his eyes shut, he felt as if someone was staring at him face to face. Even when he heard a high-pitched screaming in his ear, he screwed up his eyes as tight as he could. This occurred once a month until Markus became used to it and eventually opened his eyes – but there was nothing to see.

A FIGURE AT THE WINDOW

Then one evening Markus was standing in the driveway waiting for his friends when he happened to look up at his room and saw a figure standing in the window. It was a grim-faced old woman with long, white hair; she was wearing a nightgown. The friends saw her too. This was the first of several appearances witnessed by Markus and other visitors to the building. When Markus eventually married, his wife, who had no knowledge of the uninvited guest, saw the old woman in the window and asked who she was. 'That's Mrs Kennedy,' Markus told her, for by now he knew the old woman's identity. He had been told her name by the daughter of a neighbour who, as a child, had often seen the old woman watching her while she played in the street.

After Markus left home and his parents moved to an apartment on the lower floor, a succession of tenants moved in – and out – citing the apparition as their reason for vacating early. A curious footnote to this story is that one day, when Markus was showing photos of his old home to work colleagues, one of them recognized the building as the former care home where her mother had worked. One of her patients had been Mrs Kennedy.

HOTEL CALIFORNIA

There is nothing spookier than a derelict mental hospital – other than a haunted one. Among the more imposing of such institutions is Camarillo State Mental Hospital in California which opened in 1936 and was home to

7,000 patients, many of them violent. The hospital was reputed to be haunted by several former inmates, some of them as young as eleven years old. Many of them had allegedly been subjected to electro-shock therapy and heavy sedation. It is rumoured that abuse was endemic and several patients had been murdered by their fellow inmates. The combination of violent death, routine brutality, mind-altering drugs and mental illness is thought to account for the uncommonly large number of disturbed souls said to be haunting the corridors of this creepy facility. It is believed to have been the inspiration for the Eagles' 1976 hit 'Hotel California' (whose guests can check-out anytime, but can never leave…).

Female cleaners have reported seeing disembodied legs in the stalls of the men's toilets. Other people have been roughly manhandled by invisible hands, and had their hair pulled and their shoulders gripped and shaken. The figure of a man has been seen entering the women's restroom dressed in the tan jumpsuit that patients were required to wear to distinguish them from the staff. When Sheryl Downey, a nurse, called out to him he ignored her and went inside, so she called a co-worker, who found the room empty. The co-worker couldn't account for the sudden disappearance, as there were no windows or exits, but when he reported this to

Sheryl he saw the man standing behind her – then the man vanished.

A more humane regime was introduced at the start of the 1990s, but the facility finally closed in 1997. Still, the building retained a disturbing influence over visitors, including film crews who used it as a movie location. Actors and technicians complained of nausea, dizziness, splitting headaches and fatigue as well as an uncomfortable feeling of being watched. Tools disappeared only to reappear in locked rooms, objects fell to the floor while no one was within reach and there were sightings of a woman in white drifting through the abandoned wards and the spirit of an old woman near the bell tower. But perhaps saddest of all is the ghost of an old man who has been seen sitting at a bus stop outside the hospital, waiting for a ride that never comes.

GHOSTS OF NEW YORK

New York might seem to be too modern and bustling a city to offer ghosts the eerie quiet they seem to crave, but the Big Apple's skyscrapers and apartment blocks were erected on the site of former saloons, prohibition era speakeasies and paupers' cemeteries known as potter's fields (800,000 paupers are buried in the Bronx alone). So you just have to know where to look and which areas to stake out to catch the dead at play.

The Old Merchant's House at 29 East 4th Street is now a well-preserved museum with many interesting artifacts, but it is a melancholy place to visit after dark. For it is then that the hapless spirit of Gertrude Tredwell, spinster daughter of a wealthy businessman, walks the empty rooms. Gertrude gave birth to an infant out of wedlock and was forced to live an unhappy existence in the shadow of her domineering father.

According to the *New York Times*, the 19th-century townhouses in Bay Ridge, Brooklyn, are haunted by several restless souls who pace the corridors in the early hours, their shadows passing across the frosted glass panels in the front doors of the second-floor apartments. One tenant told reporters of the night she woke to see a figure hovering over her bed and of another occasion when she felt the ice-cold touch of phantom fingers on her back.

In a Chelsea tenement, a young golden-haired girl in a lacy dress gave the living tenant's heart a jump start when he turned over in bed to see her kneeling in prayer with her hands clasped and her head looking heavenward. As he reached to touch her hair, she vanished. The next night a man – perhaps her father – appeared in the air above a sleeping tenant and the following night the ghost of a middle-aged woman was seen staring at a blank TV screen in the same apartment, but vanished the instant the light was switched on.

Even paranormal investigators get the creeps in Bay Ridge. Arthur Matos of the Eastern Paranormal Investigation Centre confessed to being too scared to be left alone in an apartment where he had recorded the sound of a little girl humming and a husky disembodied voice asking, 'What's that?'

LOOKS LIKE TEEN SPIRIT

The Upper West Side is host to fashionable spooks, such as the Kurt Cobain lookalike in ripped jeans and grunge shirt who materialized in Ellen Giglio's apartment. He strolled across the room and melted into the wall. When Ellen described the youth to the building's superintendent he didn't doubt her story for a moment. He recognized the young man as a previous tenant who had jumped to his death from the roof wearing the very same clothes Ellen described.

The inhabitants of Morningside Heights are decidedly more retro – both the living and the dead. A demolition man and blogger who uses the moniker Bald Punk doesn't scare easily, but he resents having to share his Budweiser with an uninvited guest whose sad eyes and cadaverous features elicit pity rather than terror. But even a hard man can get shaken up when a spook drains away before his eyes, as this sad-eyed spectre did after wandering around the apartment in a fuzzy blue cloud.

THE BIG APPLE'S BIG NAMES

The Big Apple has its share of notable historical apparitions, too. The city's last Dutch colonial governor, Peter Stuyvesant (nicknamed Peg-Leg Pete after the wooden prosthesis replacing his amputated right leg) has been sighted hopping down the dimly-lit alleys of the East Village and around St Mark's in the Bowery.

The Morris-Jumel Mansion at 65 Jumel Terrace was built in 1765 for British colonel Roger Morris and it is the oldest house in Manhattan. It is rumoured to be haunted by the ghost of its former mistress, Eliza Jumel, who glides through the rooms in a purple dress checking that windows and doors are locked. There's also the restless spirit of a young suicide victim – a servant girl who jumped from an upstairs window – and a soldier of the American Revolution whose portrait hangs on display.

The spirit of author and wit Mark Twain is thought to hang out in a 19th-century brownstone building at 14 West 10th Street, where he lived briefly at the beginning of the 20th century. However, the building has a more sinister reputation on account of the twenty-two violent deaths that have occurred there in more recent years, giving rise to the unenviable nickname 'The House of Death'.

SPIRITS IN A BOTTLE

These sites don't welcome paranormal investigators or curious tourists, but if you're looking for atmosphere there are plenty of bars where you can sit over a drink as you wait for sightings of spirits of a different kind. The intimidating spectre of Welsh poet Dylan Thomas has been seen brooding at his favourite corner table at the White Horse tavern in the West Village, where he allegedly drank himself to death in 1953.

The Bridge Café at 279 Water Street under the Brooklyn Bridge is reputedly haunted by pirates who once frequented the oldest drinking den in 'New Amsterdam'. The 19th-century Landmark Tavern on 46th Street boasts the ghosts of a Confederate soldier and an Irish serving girl, while the Manhattan Bistro on 129 Spring Street was the site of a vicious murder when a young girl, Emma Sands, was dropped down a well in what is now the basement. Her alleged murderer, Levi Weeks, was not convicted and Emma is believed to be unable to rest until he confesses to the killing.

Then there is the Chelsea Hotel (immortalized in

song by Lou Reed and Leonard Cohen), where the belligerent spirit of Sid Vicious taunts the guests; and Chumleys, a speakeasy at 86 Bedford Street, where John Steinbeck, William Faulkner and F. Scott Fitzgerald enjoyed a snifter. It is also said to be haunted by Henrietta Chumley, wife of the former owner, who drinks Manhattans with lonely barflies. Another incorporeal presence in that district of the city is Thomas Jefferson's former vice president, Aaron Burr, who still frequents the quaintly named restaurant One If By Land, Two If By Sea in Barrow Street. Aaron has been seen in the company of his daughter, Theodosia, who drowned off the coast of North Carolina en route to visit her father. The building stands on the site that once was their carriage house. Female customers at the restaurant have been robbed of their earrings by the mischievous Theodosia, and plates have been sent flying by her intemperate father, who once killed a political rival in a duel.

SHOWBIZ GHOSTS

The Dakota Building at Central Park West has a morbid fascination for many, as it was both the location of John Lennon's murder and the setting for Roman Polanski's horror movie *Rosemary's Baby*. The exclusive apartment block is also known for being haunted by the spirit of a young man and a girl in turn-of-the-century dress. While Lennon's restless spirit has been sighted near the grimly named Undertaker's Gate.

The theatres of Times Square and Broadway are crowded with ghosts of performers and backstage staff. The Belasco Theatre is said to be haunted by the ghost of its eponymous owner, who died in 1931, but who returns to shake a clammy hand with unsuspecting thespians. The Public Theatre occasionally plays host to the spectre of Washington Irving, author of *The Legend of Sleepy Hollow*; and the Palace Theatre in midtown Manhattan is believed to be inhabited by more than a hundred different ghosts, which surely qualifies it as one of the most haunted buildings in New York. Judy Garland's ghost has been sighted standing by a private entrance and the vague impression of a little girl has been seen on the balcony, as has that of a small boy near the mezzanine. A phantom female cellist has been seen practising after hours in the orchestra pit and a haunting piano refrain has been heard in the auditorium, even though the piano lid is always locked when the instrument is not in use. Perhaps the most unsettling spirit is that of an acrobat who fell to his death during a performance. To see him is to be forewarned of one's own death.

Performers and backstage staff at the New Amsterdam

Theatre at 214 West 42nd Street have reason to leave immediately after the evening's entertainment. This is when the ghost of Olive Thomas, a Ziegfeld Follies chorus girl, can be encountered drifting through the auditorium, a blue bottle clutched in her shadowy hand. It is thought to be the bottle of syphilis medicine prescribed for her unfaithful alcoholic husband, from which she drank a fatal dose when his womanizing had become too much for her to bear.

One of the more bizarre residents of New York is buried in the grounds of St Paul's Chapel on Broadway and Fulton Street. English actor George Frederick Cooke died in September 1811, but he was interred without his head which he donated to science in payment of medical bills. His skull was subsequently used in several productions of *Hamlet*, although it's not known if it was acknowledged in the programme. Cooke's headless ghost is said to haunt the burial ground.

MORE CITY SPIRITS

Finally, most impressive of all is the derelict King's Park Psychiatric Centre on Long Island, with its dozens of century-old buildings that housed the seriously disturbed and criminally insane. From its abandoned buildings, shrieks and screams can be heard by those brave enough to venture within earshot.

If you imagine that you can avoid bumping into the spirits of the old city by sticking to the modern tourist sites, think again. Some visitors to the Empire State Building in Lower Manhattan have seen more than a spectacular panorama from the viewing gallery. A young woman in 1940s clothes has been heard to say that she can't live without her fiancé, who has been killed in the war. She has been seen to throw herself off the observation platform, in spite of the high safety barriers (which were not in place till after the Second World War). There's no need to rush to see this performance, as she repeats it every night.

HAUNTED LONDON THEATRES

While stately homes and castles are still the most popular 'haunt' for restless spirits, theatres must surely rank in the top five. As every theatregoer knows, it's hard to get an actor to leave the stage after the final curtain – but it's even more difficult when they are dead!

London lays claim to being the most haunted city in the world. The cluster of theatres concentrated in the West End date back to the Elizabethan era, so it's not surprising that there are reputed to be hundreds of deceased actors, directors and backstage employees who refuse to leave the spotlight.

OUT FOR THE COUNT

In 1878, actor-manager Sir Henry Irving acquired the lease of the Lyceum Theatre in the Strand and brought in his business manager, Bram Stoker. In his office, over a seven-year period, Stoker wrote much of *Dracula* and, like many literary and artistic figures of the 19th century, is believed to have indulged in opium to stimulate his imagination. Opium is said to stimulate the psychic senses, or Third Eye, located in the pineal gland near the centre of the brain. This produces melatonin, a hormone that affects sleep patterns. Under the influence of drugs, Stoker's intense brooding on the dark subject matter of his novel and his research into the myth of vampirism over such a protracted period may have created the etheric equivalent of a wormhole through which spirits pass from their dimension to our own. That's a theory put forward by psychic investigator Becky Walsh and her team, who held a vigil in the upper circle bar in 2005. They sensed a 'sweeping energy' which left them all feeling nauseous and which they attributed to a past resident having dabbled in the occult.

Stoker's ghost has not been seen in the theatre, although an assistant manager reported being surprised by a man who walked out of a solid wall near the grand circle, tipped his hat and bid the startled employee 'good morning' before vanishing.

The ghost of a grey lady has been seen by several staff members and their descriptions of her bear an uncanny resemblance to the photograph of actress Ellen Terry which hangs in the box office. Ellen's spirit was seen by an employee at an hour when the building would have been empty. She was dressed in a grey cloak and ignored his pleas to stop, so he followed her down a corridor until she disappeared into the solid wall at the far end.

THE SHOW MUST GO ON

The spirit of rock star Freddie Mercury has been seen by several employees at the Dominion Theatre, Tottenham Court Road, where the Queen musical *We Will Rock You* has been packing them in since May 2002. Cast member Jenna Lee James claims to have felt Freddie pass through her as she was singing one of his songs, while Ian John Shillito, stage manager and co-author of *Haunted West End Theatres*, remembers sensing a presence while cueing the show. He then saw Freddie watching from the wings and criticizing aspects he didn't approve of!

The aptly named Phoenix Theatre in Charing Cross Road is rumoured to be haunted by the ghost of musical star Stephanie Lawrence, who is best remembered for creating the roles of Pearl in *Starlight Express* and Mrs

Johnstone in the musical *Blood Brothers*. She died in November 2000, but deputy stage manager Richard Kingcott 'saw' her twelve years later, standing in a doorway of the set in her costume as if awaiting her entrance. At first Kingcott thought nothing of it, as he had been accustomed to seeing her there when she was alive, but he then realized that of course she was dead.

Stephanie isn't the only cast member Kingcott has witnessed returning to the scene of a former triumph. On several occasions, when a character known as Eddie has been on stage, Kingcott has felt a presence behind him. He believes it is that of a young cast member who died tragically while essaying the role. Stage manager and psychic investigator Becky Walsh also sensed a presence behind her when she worked at the Phoenix. It only occurred when the character of Eddie was on stage and usually when an understudy was taking the role, which suggested that the young actor who had died was checking out his replacement. Becky gave a detailed description of the young man to the company manager, who confirmed that it was an accurate description of the youth who had died while playing the part of Eddie.

It is ironic that the Fortune Theatre in Covent Garden was haunted by a ghost during a long-running production of the supernatural thriller *The Woman in*

135

Black. The most unnerving aspect was that the real apparition and the stage spectre looked uncannily alike, prompting other cast members to do a double-take. Natalie Block, an usher turned actress who had taken the role of the ghost, saw her doppelganger on several occasions. Some years ago, Natalie was sitting at the back of the dress circle during a performance when she noticed a grey shadow in box A. She turned away, thinking it was a trick of the light, but when she looked again the shadow had form. It was clearly a woman and she was sitting motionless watching the play, wearing a turn-of-the-century corseted dress with her hair done in a fashionable Victorian style. Natalie looked away, wondering if the vision would have vanished when she looked back, and sure enough the box was empty.

When the theatre management heard about the sighting they immediately saw the opportunity for publicity and informed the press that a real ghost was watching the show. Natalie had also sensed an oppressive atmosphere in the small hospitality room attached to Box A and smelt perfume and pipe smoke in other parts of the building. She claims that while she was on stage she had seen a 'moving darkness' in the wings and that the young male lead had experienced considerable anxiety as he watched her walk off stage into the outstretched arms of the ghost! Natalie insists she saw nothing on that occasion, but felt her skin crawl when she was told about it later.

THE BALLET GHOST

The Palace Theatre on Shaftesbury Avenue is home to a curious apparition – the torso of a ballerina which emerges from the floor of the stage to perform an arabesque. It is believed to be the world famous ballet dancer Anna Pavlova, who appeared regularly on the bill when the theatre was known as the Palace of Varieties. The reason why only her upper body is seen is that, in Pavlova's time, the stage was at a lower level.

THE ARISTOCRAT AND THE CLOWN

The oldest theatre in the West End is the Theatre Royal, Drury Lane, which is thought to date back to the 17th century. Perhaps unsurprisingly it is considered to host more ghosts than its neighbours. Its most famous inhabitant is an 18th-century aristocrat known to past and present members of the cast and crew as the 'Man in Grey'. This gentleman always appears in a powdered wig and a tricorne hat, immaculately attired in a jacket, cloak and riding boots and carrying a sword. He is believed to be the ghost of a murder victim whose remains were discovered bricked up within the building, a knife protruding from his ribs. His manifestation during rehearsal is possibly the best-documented sighting of its type, as he was witnessed by the entire cast. Unfortunately, no one had the presence of mind to ask for his autograph!

Those suffering from coulrophobia (fear of clowns) would do well to avoid visiting the Theatre Royal, as the mischievous spirit of Joseph Grimaldi, the 'father' of modern clowns, has an unnerving habit of appearing behind members of the audience dressed in full white face make-up. There is surely only one thing more scary than a clown close up and that's a dead clown breathing down your neck! Grimaldi has been credited with guiding nervous actors through their paces, but is less gracious with the more experienced members of the company. Many have complained of being kicked by an invisible mischief-maker and theatre legend has it that the head of the old joker has been seen to manifest in the mirror of his old dressing room, to the consternation of any poor actor who happens to be applying his make-up at the time.

WILLY WONKA'S GHOST

The Aldwych Theatre in Drury Lane was built by actor-manager Seymour Hicks and opened in 1905. In the 1920s it became famous for presenting a series of popular comedies known as the *Aldwych Farces*, but there have been few laughs for the staff who have complained of poltergeist activity such as doors opening unaided, the sound of a woman weeping and spirit lights or orbs floating through the auditorium. As might be expected, the turnover in staff is uncommonly high.

When psychic Becky Walsh investigated the Aldwych, she 'saw' clairvoyantly the image of a gentleman dressed in what she described as a Willy Wonka-style costume with a top hat and cane. She sensed that the ghost's manner of dress was not in keeping with the period, but reflected instead his eccentric fashion sense and style. She had the impression that he had been a wealthy entrepreneur who had renovated the theatre and considered it his 'baby'. She believed that at some point he had sold the theatre and she was watching him walking from the building for the last time. She reported her findings to the management, who produced a photograph of Seymour Hicks dressed in what can only be described as a Willy Wonka costume of the kind worn by Johnny Depp in the Tim Burton movie, *Charlie and the Chocolate Factory*.

THE OLD VIC

The Old Vic derives its name from the Royal Victoria Coffee and Music Hall established in 1880 by social reformer Emma Cons. Miss Cons is said to haunt the theatre along with her niece Lilian Baylis, who took over the management of the theatre when her aunt died in 1912. Lilian has been seen on the balcony of the upper circle staring wistfully out of the window at the garden across the road.

The lady with bloodstained hands who has been seen by many over the years is thought to be the spirit of a Shakespearean actress reliving her role in 'the Scottish play'. (The title of *Macbeth* is never to be mentioned backstage for fear of bringing a curse on the production.) One evening, stage doorman Ned Sego saw the actress on the second floor as he was checking the building was empty before locking up for the night. He assumed she was an actress because she was wearing period costume and looked as solid as the rest of the company he had just seen leave the theatre, but as he followed closely behind her down the stairs to the exit she disappeared through a bricked-up doorway which must have been the exit in former times. Ned admitted that at that moment his heart stopped.

After the First World War the company was performing *Julius Caesar*; it featured a cast that had been assembled in some haste as several leading players had died in the Spanish Flu epidemic of 1918. On the opening night, some members of the company asked the director who the 'extra' was in the orchard scene. The director didn't recognize the man so he asked a friend, who unhesitatingly identified him as Eric Moss, the actor who had taken the part of Brutus before succumbing to a fatal bout of the flu.

LES MISERABLES

The Queen's Theatre in Soho, London is perhaps best known by contemporary theatregoers as the venue for *Les Misérables*, but its hundred-year history has produced a number of ghost stories. Chief electrician Mike Cordina spotted what he thought was a contractor passing through the upper circle of the auditorium after everyone had gone home. The exits were locked and chained, leaving only the Stage Door unlocked, so Mike was concerned that the man, who had short grey hair and was dressed in a long grey coat with velvet lapels, would lose his way looking for a way out. He called out to him, but the man continued walking and disappeared round a corner – literally, it seems, for as soon as Mike rounded the corner he came to a solid, blank wall. The stranger was nowhere to be seen.

Other members of staff have reported seeing the same figure when the building was known to be empty, and Becky Walsh has sensed the presence of a male spirit standing behind her when working as a member of the staff at the theatre. On that occasion she mentally asked the spirit to identify himself and was told clairvoyantly that he had worked in the office situated through a door at the back of the auditorium. This was curious because there was no door there. A week or so later, Becky happened to see an old photograph of the theatre and there was indeed a door precisely where the ghost had described it.

THE STRANGLER JACKET

The Duke of York's Theatre in Saint Martin's Lane is home to the ghost of another actor-manager, Violet Melonette, who died in 1935. She has been sighted in the audience on a number of occasions, although it's not known if she voiced her opinion of the show she was watching or simply gave patrons the cold shoulder. The theatre, which opened in 1892, also houses a singular item of macabre memorabilia – a lady's bolero jacket that has been known to drive its wearers to question their own sanity. It originally belonged to Victorian actress Edith Merryweather, who was allegedly drowned by a jealous lover. It is said that the jacket was bought on a market stall and worn by various actresses, all of whom complained of feeling constricted, to the extent that the garment quickly acquired the name 'the Strangler Jacket'. Subsequently, actresses refused to wear it. In an effort to allay their fears, the wife of the then producer volunteered to try it on. She reluctantly admitted that it seemed to contract as soon as she buttoned it up, making it hard to breathe. On handing the jacket back to the wardrobe mistress, the producer's wife saw a look on the poor woman's face that made her wish she had taken the story more seriously. For on the producer's wife's neck, clear for all to see, was a red band of welts such as might have been made by a strangler's hands.

THE SPOOK WITH CHUBBY CHEEKS

The 300-year-old Theatre Royal, Haymarket, is reputed to be haunted by comic actor-manager John Baldwin Buckstone, whose disembodied voice and footsteps have been heard in what was once his dressing room. The late Margaret Rutherford (cinema's original Miss Marple) and her dresser once spent the night in that very room and claim to have seen Buckstone's spirit enter, only to vanish before their eyes.

In 1949, Sir Donald Sinden was appearing in a play with Sir Ralph Richardson when he and actress Gillian Howell saw a man in a long, grey Victorian morning coat standing near Richardson's dressing room. The man looked pensive and was staring out of the window. He had his back to them so they both assumed that it was

Richardson; they greeted him as they passed on their way to the stage, but received no reply. A few minutes later, as they waited in the wings, they saw Richardson on stage, so Sinden rushed back up the stairs to check, but the mysterious figure had vanished. More recently, Dame Judi Dench saw a man in a long tailcoat hurrying ahead of her along the corridor from the stage to the auditorium, but when she turned the corner she came to a dead end and he was nowhere to be seen.

The ghost may have been Buckstone, who was also seen by the theatre's master carpenter one night long after the evening performance had finished. The phantom was dressed in a cloak and top hat, but what is particularly significant about this sighting is that the witness remarked on the spirit's solidity and that it vanished in front of him. This gave the carpenter such a fright that it made him physically ill. The carpenter recalled that the ghost had been smiling and had 'chubby cheeks' and he identified the spectre as Buckstone from a photograph in the archives.

Sometimes the spooks are not so solid. One staff member was pursued by two shadows as she walked down a backstage passageway. One was her own; but the other continued past her when she stopped to see who was following her.

Stage doorman Brian Russell believes he made

physical contact with a ghost when he went under the stage to turn off the lights and collided with what he described as an 'electric energy' so strong that it made him nauseous.

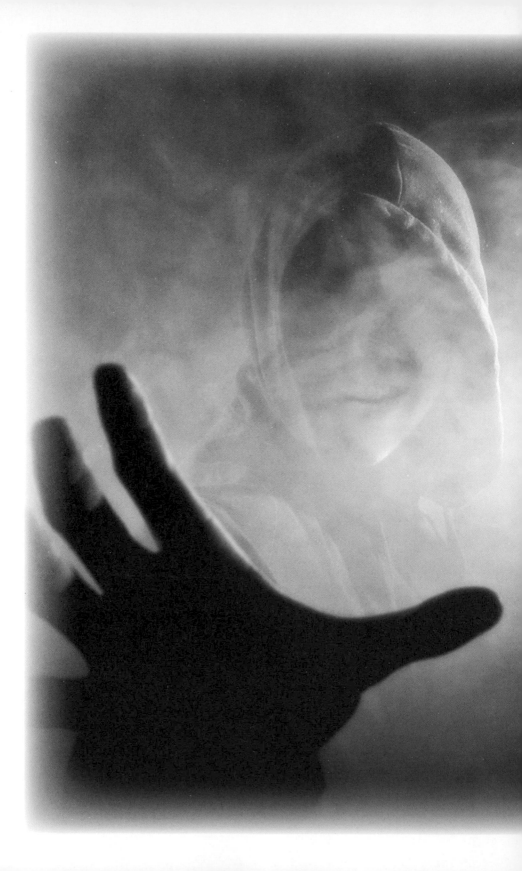

4

THE
LIVING
DEAD

Ghosts aren't what they used to be. Nor
are they always where you would expect
to find them. They're everywhere
and they have no respect for privacy or
personal property. They can make your
life hell – literally. The nasty ones have
been known to take possession of you
if they really want to mess you up, and
when they do, you'll have the devil of
a job evicting them. However, not all
ghosts are up to mischief. If some
of the cases in this chapter are to be
believed, a few ghosts may even have
a social conscience.

In 2008, Nita Hickok was travelling through Utah en route to Idaho at night with her partner Mike, who had offered to share the driving, when they noticed a motorcycle some distance behind them. Its headlight was flickering as though it was faulty, so the pair thought they ought to slow down in case the rider wanted to follow close behind and benefit from their headlights. Then suddenly the motorbike was alongside them and to their horror they saw that both rider and bike had been in a serious accident. The rider was wearing ripped leathers and the bike, an old Harley, was severely damaged. Nita and Mike were convinced the rider was a dead man. But he was pointing to the side of the road as if trying to get them to pull over. They did so, but Mike lost his nerve and scrambled over into the passenger seat yelling at Nita to take the wheel. She wriggled over into the driver's seat, but refused to drive on. In the distance she could see two trucks racing each other side by side and a few moments later they roared past leaving the terrified couple now grateful they had seen the ghost rider. They are certain they heard his voice inside the car telling them he had been driven off the road and saying that his body had lain undiscovered in a sugar beet field for several days.

It sounds like a typical urban legend, or a scene from *Ghost Rider*, but there are countless stories of people who have survived certain death because of what they believe to have been intervention by invisible entities. Some of these experiences have even been corroborated by several witnesses.

GHOST IN A HARD HAT

In the late 1960s, a Jacksonville newspaper reported that an elementary school teacher and her class had narrowly escaped death or serious injury thanks to a mysterious visitor. The man, who claimed to be part of a construction crew working on the school grounds, had entered the classroom dressed in overalls and wearing a hard hat. He had told the teacher that his men would be working just outside that morning and it would be very noisy, so she might want to take the children into the playground. Moments after the children had filed out, part of the roof collapsed, but thanks to the mystery man no one was injured. As soon as she had recovered from the shock the teacher tried to find the man to thank him, but he was nowhere to be found. The principal called the construction company and gave them a description of the man, but they had no record of him.

The following sounds like another campfire yarn, but those who circulate it insist that it actually happened.

SAVE MY BABY

A married couple were travelling across the United States when they were flagged down by a woman in obvious distress who appealed to them for help. She told them that she had been in a traffic accident and that her husband was dead, but their newborn baby was still alive and trapped in their car which had run off the road into a ditch. She was bruised and bleeding, so the wife tried to calm and comfort her while the husband hurried to the scene of the accident further on up the road. In the wreckage he saw two bodies held in their seats by seatbelts and found the baby crying in the back. He carried it to his car, where he thought the mother would be waiting, but she was gone. His wife insisted that the woman had followed him to the scene of the accident, but he hadn't seen her there. So he left the infant with his wife and went back to the wreck. Looking inside, he now saw that the female passenger was the very same woman who had asked him to save her baby.

THE RAILWAY CROSSING

In San Antonio, Texas, it is said that the Villamain Road railway crossing is haunted by the spirits of several children who were killed by a freight train after their school bus stalled on the tracks. Legend has it that these same children can be counted on to push a vehicle free if it stalls on the line.

Some people laugh it off as yet another urban myth (claiming that the tragedy occurred in another state). But others swear they have tested the claims by deliberately driving on to the railway tracks at this particular crossing, putting their vehicle in neutral and waiting for invisible hands to push them clear of an oncoming train (not something we would recommend!). Those who survived this dangerous and reckless stunt swore that after they had safely reached the other side they found children's handprints on the rear of their vehicles. Many locals have even gone to the length of having their cars and trucks cleaned and then dusted with talcum powder to be sure of preserving the tiny prints.

THE GRAY MAN

Less dramatic, but equally intriguing, is the legend of the Gray Man of Pawley's Island, South Carolina. Local legend has it that he always appears before a hurricane and those who see him are fortunate because it means their house will escape undamaged. One of the worst storms on record to hit the island was Hurricane Hugo in the early 1990s. Shortly afterwards, national TV reports stated that only those residents who claimed to have seen the Gray Man shortly before the storm struck had a home to go back to. It is believed he was either the son of the owner of the local hotel, the Pelican Inn, or a young man who suffered a fatal fall from his horse while out riding across the sands with his fiancée shortly before their wedding.

A TIMELY INTERVENTION

Some individuals claim to have been saved from harm by spectral Good Samaritans, but we are asked to take their accounts on trust.

A young woman in California, who wishes to remain anonymous, told the website yourghoststories.com that after escaping a violent relationship in 2007 she shared an apartment with a man she had known for many years. At that time, her new flatmate was still mourning the loss of his sister, Lucy, and had made a small shrine to her memory in a bookcase. This housed poems his sister had written, together with photographs, candles and a glass cross. Every morning they would drink to Lucy's memory and play her favourite song. For that, the flatmate promised that Lucy would protect anyone who lived in the apartment.

One night, while the man was at work, the young woman's ex-boyfriend phoned and demanded to see her. She refused and, without thinking, blurted out that he would have to wait until Lucy's brother returned from work if he wanted to come to the apartment. Now the ex-boyfriend knew that she was alone. He also knew where the apartment was because he had been the brother's friend. The young woman said her ex-boyfriend found a way in to the apartment and attempted to rape her at knife-point. But she claimed that the bookcase started to shake, the candles were snuffed out, the glass cross fell, hitting her attacker on the back, and the record player came on by itself, blasting out Lucy's favourite song. Startled, the boyfriend fled and was never seen again.

To the rationally minded, it would seem more likely that the violent motion of the sofa on which the attack took place caused the bookcase to shake and the cross to topple, but for the traumatized young woman it felt as though she had been saved by the spirit of the apartment's previous occupant. But who can say for sure?

SMOKE IN THE KITCHEN

The yourghoststories.com website also offers a near-death experience contributed by Spore from Canada.

She describes being home alone one day and deciding to make pop tarts, which should be heated in a toaster. Mistakenly, however, she put them in the microwave. Then she went back to watching TV in the next room.

She was standing in the doorway with her back to the kitchen when she felt someone run behind her; her hair stood on end. There was no one else in the house and no draught that could account for the sensation. The windows were closed and the air conditioning and fans were all switched off. Spinning round to see who it was, she saw that the kitchen was now filled with smoke and the microwave was sparking.

'I guess this was a ghost trying to tell me what was happening behind my back and save my life and my house. I've always believed in ghosts and spirits, but when I actually felt one run behind me and blow my hair up I was more of a believer.'

A WARNING VOICE

Forty-year-old Lakota (her pen name) remembers the ghostly voice that saved her from what she believes could have been a traumatic abduction.

When she was in her early teens in the mid-1980s she often played with her dog, Dasha, around what had once been coal mines near her home in the north of England. One summer evening she was returning from the fields and was waiting by the side of the road for a gap in the traffic. She was about to cross when she heard a voice whisper in her ear, 'Watch out for the next car that comes over the brow of the hill!'

'I was… stunned. No one stood on the pavement next to me and I instinctively knew this voice was a message. At such a young age, "brow" wasn't a word I'd use.'

Lakota was puzzled as to why she had been warned about a car she couldn't see. But she stepped back from the verge and, although there was now a gap in the traffic, she did not cross. Then a car came over the hill from her right. It slowed down as it approached and she caught a glimpse of the driver's face. He was middle-aged and there was something in his look that unsettled her.

'The driver pulled in at the kerb, level with me. He then leaned across and flung his passenger door open, his arm stretched out as if to grab me. I panicked, but this ghostly whisper had given me a head start.'

Seeing a car parked in one of the driveways to her left, she made a run for the house and banged on the window, calling for help. A couple came out and, when they heard the girl's story, the husband went to confront the driver who was still sitting in his car which was now parked at the end of their drive with the passenger door open. 'The man from the house got angry with him and I remember him swearing a lot. The driver quickly shut his car door and sped away.

'The woman of the house kindly walked me back home and explained to my terrified parents what had happened. I was so grateful to these people who had assisted me out of danger and assured my safety, but even more grateful to this ghostly voice who had warned me about the car that was yet to appear at that point. I dread to think what would have happened if I hadn't had this warning and wonder if I'd have still been alive today.'

A MIRACULOUS ESCAPE

Ghostly warning voices are believed to be an individual's guardian angel, or all-knowing 'higher self', depending on whether you subscribe to the spiritual or the psychological view, but if you recognize the voice as belonging to someone who has passed over, then there can't be much doubt about it.

In February 1999, the Sarasota *Herald-Tribune* reported that local resident Maria Tejada had narrowly escaped certain death. A car had crashed through the door of her home in Florida, flattening the sofa she had been sitting in only moments before. The car was driven by a teenager who had lost control of the vehicle and who would most likely have spent the rest of his life in prison if the crash had proven fatal. Maria attributed her miraculous escape to a warning given by the ghost of her dead father whose voice she had heard telling her to stand up.

The woman in the walker

They say that 'seeing is believing', and while you might dismiss a ghostly warning voice as a figment of your imagination, you're more likely to take that warning seriously if it's delivered 'in person'.

Nevaeh is a film producer living in San Francisco; she is also a psychic. In 2009, she was looking forward to staying at the Algonquin Hotel in New York City, which is reputedly haunted by the ghost of writer and socialite Dorothy Parker. But it wasn't Dorothy's ghost Nevaeh saw in her hotel suite that first night – it was an old woman in a walker. The woman appeared at the end of Nevaeh's bed and told her, 'Stay on course... go home, go straight home.'

Normally Nevaeh would have checked out there and then, but she planned to visit Buffalo to see her ailing elderly aunt Ann, who she hadn't seen for a long time, and wanted to take the opportunity of a cheap connecting flight. Nevaeh felt terrible about cancelling the visit and disappointing her aunt, but as if to answer her thoughts the ghost added, 'She'll forgive you… go straight home.'

With a heavy heart, Nevaeh called her aunt to say that she wouldn't be able to visit. Aunt Ann was bitterly disappointed and would not be consoled by her niece's promise to visit in six months or a year. 'I'll be dead then,' she said.

As she was checking out of the hotel next morning, Nevaeh saw the old lady in the walker again. The woman waved goodbye and said, 'I'll see you next time.'

By the time Nevaeh arrived at the airport, her psychic senses were quickened.

'I felt an explosion, people screaming, metal crunching. My associates watched me sweat and run to the ladies' room. I had a premonition. I knew something was wrong — everything was wrong.'

On board the plane, she was overcome with anxiety and couldn't help confiding her fears to an associate travelling with her. It was a dreadful flight, as the plane was buffeted by bad weather, but Nevaeh was no longer afraid. She knew she would survive because the ghost at the Algonquin had told her she would be returning to the hotel. So why had she experienced such anxiety at the airport? The next day, the answer came. The evening news reported a plane crash in Buffalo – it was the very same plane Nevaeh had been scheduled to take to visit her aunt. There were no survivors.

HIT AND RUN

Some spirits relive the moment of their death time and again as if they can't accept that they are no longer living. But if it's tough on the deceased, imagine what it must be like for the poor motorist who runs over a ghost!

On the A435 in Warwickshire, England, a phantom cyclist has been giving drivers a fright. A father and son were driving past Coughton Court, the ancestral home of the Throckmorton family, when a young woman wearing a white plastic raincoat and riding a bicycle suddenly appeared in front of their car, giving the father no time to brake. Instinctively he veered to one side and crashed through some garden railings. Neither driver nor passenger had heard or felt a collision, but they knew they couldn't have avoided hitting the cyclist. The father got out of the car to see if anything could be done for the woman, but there was no sign of her body or the bike.

After much frantic searching, he went to a nearby house and roused the owner, explaining as calmly as he could that he had just run someone over and needed to call an ambulance. To his surprise, the householder seemed amused rather than alarmed. 'Was she wearing a white mac?' he asked. And when the

Above: The Spectors Investigations Crew from the US TV show *Ghost Hunters.*

Above: An investigator uses a zircon meter to detect metal and electricity which he believes help to indicate signs of paranormal activity.

Above: The Myrtles, a haunted plantation house in St Francisville, Louisiana.

Above: The Old Vic theatre in London is haunted by the ghost of an actor who died during the flu epidemic of 1918.

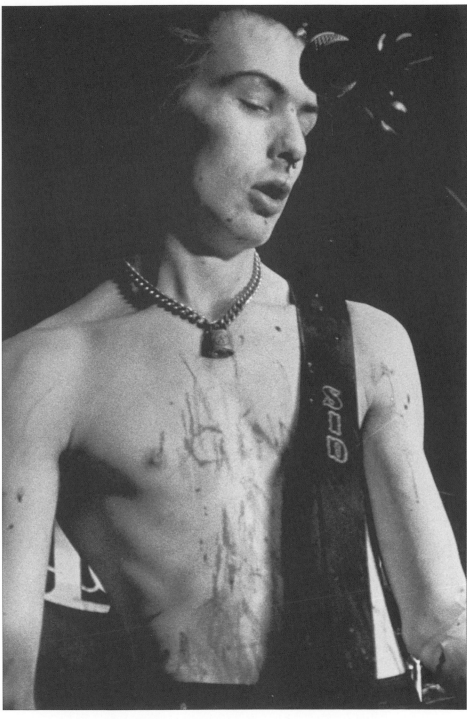

Above: In October 1978, a distraught Sid Vicious of punk band the Sex Pistols was found in Room 100 of the Chelsea Hotel with the body of his girlfriend, Nancy Spungen. Vicious died of a heroin overdose in February the following year. His ghost is said to harass visitors to the hotel.

Above: Freddie Mercury of the rock group Queen, whose spirit is said to watch over performers at the Dominion Theatre in London.

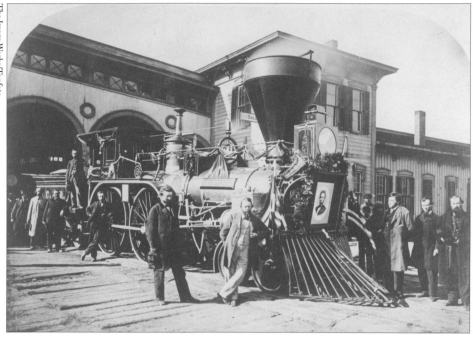

Above: Abraham Lincoln's funeral train with a portrait of the President mounted on the front of the engine. Does a spectral locomotive still mark Lincoln's final journey from Washington, D. C. to Springfield?

Left: The notorious Judge Jeffreys, 'the hanging judge' who presided over the 'Bloody Assizes' in late 17th-century Britain in which about three hundred rebels against King James II were sentenced to death.

Above: The Angel of Mons tells of a group of heavenly soldiers who protected British forces at the Battle of Mons. Some think the tale was a propaganda tool which served to boost the Allies' morale during the First World War.

Above: Many people believe we each have a spirit double (the astral soul referred to in Hindu and Tibetan traditions) which can be released naturally and spontaneously when we are in a deep state of relaxation, most commonly during sleep.

Above: General George S. Patton was not the most obvious candidate for psychic visitations, but apparently had a number of paranormal experiences in times of battle.

Above: Visitors and staff at this old pub in Birmingham, UK, have reported assaults by a bottom-pinching ghost. Paula Wharton, assistant manager at the Queen's Arms, initially believed the tweaks were muscle spasms. But it seems the experience was not unique to her. 'One night three of us were talking,' she said, 'and I mentioned that I'd felt this pinch on my bum, and everyone else said that it had happened to them too!'

poor man nodded, the householder calmly told him to forget all about the incident as it was the fourth 'fatal' accident the cyclist had survived that week!

ACCIDENTS WILL HAPPEN… MORE THAN ONCE

When police were called to the scene of a serious accident on the Portsmouth–London Road near Guildford, Surrey, they expected to find wreckage and a driver either dead or in urgent need of an ambulance. But there was nothing to indicate that a fatal crash had occurred, not even the vehicle's skid marks where several passing motorists had seen it veer off the road and down an embankment. It was a fine, late-summer evening and visibility was good. Witnesses told the police that the car's headlights had been full on, so they could not have imagined it or mistaken it for a speeding vehicle that might have narrowly escaped the crash and driven on.

On searching the area, the police found the remains of a wrecked car nose down in a ditch, partially hidden in the undergrowth. The lights were extinguished, rust had discoloured the bodywork and the driver was long past saving. An autopsy indicated that the 21-year-old driver had died several months earlier. He had last been seen alive on 16 July and his family had reported him missing that month.

Police sergeant Russ Greenhouse told reporters, 'The car had obviously been there for a long time and thousands of motorists will have passed the spot every day. The car was discovered as a result of a report from members of the public who thought they saw a car's headlights veering off the road. The officers could not identify that collision, but they had the presence of mind to search on foot and they found this car.'

Sergeant Greenhouse would not comment when asked if the police had opened an X-file on the incident.

PHANTOM PLANES AND TRAINS, SPOOKY CARS AND VANISHING VANS

Sightings of phantom planes, trains and road vehicles are not uncommon and have been reported in almost every country in the world. But no one has offered a plausible theory as to how inanimate objects can manifest, when only the dead driver, passengers or crew are thought capable of materialization. Could it be that the witnesses are getting a glimpse of a past event that has imprinted itself on the ether at the moment of a tragedy?

In 1971, Glyn Jones was driving home around midnight after finishing work as a chef in the English village of Clare in Suffolk when he heard a loud droning sound. He pulled over to see what it could be. Looking up at the night sky, he saw a formation of more than thirty Second World War bombers heading in the same direction. During the war, this part of eastern England was an assembly area for Allied Bomber Command, and from here British and American forces launched air raids on strategic targets in Germany. But Glyn knew that by 1971 only half-a-dozen of the aircraft used for these bombing raids would still have been airworthy and they would have been scattered around the world. He hadn't been drinking or taking drugs and could only assume he had been granted a glimpse of the past, accompanied by the sound of those long-silenced engines.

In the 1980s, three passengers in a sedan (location unknown) experienced a near miss with a grey van that headed straight for them before it disappeared. Around the same time, a British driver swerved to avoid a truck that vanished as suddenly as it had appeared. A similar incident is said to have occurred in Kaniva, Australia, where a green 1940s model 'big rig' truck was said to drive straight through terrified motorists. In New Jersey, traumatized drivers complained to police of being tailgated by a demonic truck which pursued them the length of Clinton Road only to vanish as soon as they hit the main highway. And a ghost number 7 bus is known to have caused a number of accidents, one of them fatal, at the junction of St Mark's Road and

Cambridge Gardens in Notting Hill, London. The bus failed to reappear after the road was straightened.

In 1995, a Cincinnati college student was driving through town along a stretch of road with a long history of fatal accidents when he noticed a rusty light brown car of a type that was popular in the 1970s. It had distinctive bumper stickers and was making a loud noise from a damaged exhaust. The old car was cruising slowly, so the impatient student overtook and watched it fade into the distance in his rear-view mirror. But when he stopped at the next set of traffic lights, the car was there again in front of him. The student looked across at the driver and saw a skinny teenager dressed in black, with short black hair. He was staring straight ahead, hands gripping the wheel and he didn't sweat although he was wearing a thick black jumper in the 80F heat. But the strangest thing was that he was immobile and his face bore no expression. He didn't even blink.

Overtaking the rust-bucket for a second time, the student kept an eye on it in his rear-view mirror. Again it faded from view, but it appeared once more at the next set of lights. At this point it occurred to the student that this teenager could have been killed in an accident on this stretch of road. The student slowed down to see how the mystery driver would negotiate a dead man's curve in the road ahead. To his astonishment, the teenager remained motionless as the car snaked round the treacherous bend. 'It was like the driver was frozen in time, like a 3D photograph... the whole thing really gave me the creeps.'

Perhaps the most convincing evidence of a phantom vehicle was caught on film by police in Garden City, Georgia and featured on the Syfy Channel's Paranormal Files. It showed a police chase in which a white car was being driven at inhuman speeds; it then tore through a chainlink fence without breaking it.

GHOST TRAIN

In Saskatchewan, ghost-hunters gather at night along the abandoned railroad line between Prince Albert and St Louis in the hope of seeing a ghost train known locally as the St Louis Light. But the most famous ghost train in America is Abraham Lincoln's funeral train, which is said to travel from Washington, D.C. to Springfield, Illinois, on the anniversary of Lincoln's death. The train is believed to cause watches and clocks to stop at the moment of its passing.

A GROUP HAUNT

Most spectral sightings are of individual apparitions, but some have reported seeing ghostly groups assembled at sites of historical significance. As it is unlikely that individuals would share the same fate after death, these rare sightings suggest the group is merely an echo in the ether. This would explain why these apparitions do not acknowledge the living.

Three kilometres (2 miles) from the English city of Oxford is the village of Iffley, which boasts a parish church, St Mary's, dating back to Norman times. One day, a woman named Gladys and her widowed mother visited the church. While they were standing in the churchyard, the choir walked past them and went inside. There were about a dozen members of various ages and they were all wearing cassocks. The two women entered the church through the main doors, hoping to hear the choristers practise, but the place was empty. They knew the building very well, so were certain that there was no vestry or secret room where the choir could be hiding. Returning to the churchyard, they took a closer look at the point where the choir had entered the church and discovered that it was a solid wall – there was no door. When the vicar heard this story, he explained that there had once been a door there and the choir had always used it because there was no vestry or other room for them to change in the church.

A FANCY-DRESS PARTY

An elderly guest at a hotel in the English town of Shrewsbury, Shropshire, complained to the owner that she hadn't realized he would be catering for a fancy-dress party or she wouldn't have made a booking for that weekend. When he assured her he wasn't planning to host such an event and had no idea what she was referring to, she told him about the troop of Roman soldiers she had just passed on the road to the hotel. It was then he confessed that he had seen them too, some years earlier in April 1995, when he had awoken at 4.30am to prepare breakfast for the guests. Looking out of his bedroom window, he had seen a number of men talking animatedly on the front lawn. His initial thought had been that some of the guests must have risen unusually early – but then he noticed that they were all dressed as Roman soldiers and carrying spears and shields. Before he could investigate, the phone rang and he ran to answer it. By the time he went outside to investigate, the men had gone and he thought no more about it.

Six months later, the hotel owner stayed up later than usual to welcome a couple of guests who were expected to check in around 11pm. When they arrived, one of the guests said she had just seen a group of men dressed as Roman soldiers talking in the driveway. It transpired that an old Roman road runs through the grounds of the hotel. Wroxeter, the third-largest Roman city in Britain, is only 11 km (7 miles) southwest of Shrewsbury.

WALKING THE DOGS

The previous incident is a good example of a sighting that was shared by three individuals on separate occasions. But individuals have also reported simultaneous sightings that differ significantly from one another, raising the possibility that the nature of the appearance is determined by the witnesses' sensitivity to the energies they encounter.

In the winter of 1994, Tracey and her friend Jane were walking their dogs near the Worcestershire village of Kempsey. It was a bright, starry night and both women were in a relaxed and cheerful mood. But then Tracey felt a prickly sensation as if she were being watched and saw a featureless, black figure leaning against a farm gate a few metres ahead. She later described it as a 'void' which blocked out everything behind it. Although she couldn't make out the face she felt the figure was a man, who watched them as they passed.

Curiously, Jane saw the same figure in more detail. She described him as a Victorian farm labourer, about thirty-five years old, with dark hair and a cheeky grin. His cap was set at an angle and he was wearing a neckerchief and hobnailed boots. She remembered him distinctly and said he looked 'perfectly real'. But after the two women passed him, they looked back and he had gone.

A FINAL VISIT

Sometimes spirits aren't seen, but their presence can be felt. An empathic person can sense the sadness that accompanies a spirit's visit to its former home.

A young woman from Worcestershire was staying with her family in a beautiful thatched cottage in Cornwall, where she had enjoyed several happy holidays in the past. But on this occasion she couldn't shrug off an oppressive feeling of melancholia, although she had no reason to feel unhappy. All week she felt an unseen presence hovering in the house. It had a sadness about it, but the woman also felt it was pleased to have a family staying there. At the end of the week, just prior to the woman's departure, a funeral procession passed through the village. Next day, the woman asked the cleaner if she knew whose funeral it had been. The cleaner replied it was that of the old woman who had owned the cottage; she had died in a nursing home in the knowledge that her cottage was to be put up for sale and would no longer be let as a holiday home.

SPIRITS IN THE STONES

It is said that some ghosts are drawn to locations which had a special significance for them in life, particularly if a ghost's life ended in sudden or violent death in a certain place. If the connection is particularly strong, a 'recording' of the event will be embedded in the fabric of the building (something known as the 'stone tape' theory). If materials from the 'ghost' building are then used in another building, the ghost will be seen at the new location.

A hotel in Coleraine, Londonderry, Northern Ireland, had been built with timbers taken from Derry Castle, which was reputed to be haunted. Guests complained of being kept awake at night by a swishing sound. This, the hotel staff explained, was the rustling of a gown worn by the resident ghost, a young woman whose fiancé had been killed in the castle. Such ghostly phenonema were only witnessed in the hotel rooms that contained wood from the castle. The night porter subsequently resigned his position after being followed into the bar by an apparition. Earlier, he had seen a ghost walk through the locked door to one of the rooms, and had startled one of the guests by banging on the door and shouting 'I know you're in there, come on out!' However, the most disturbing sighting was experienced by a young mother. She entered her bedroom to find her two children playing with a ghost.

THE DEPARTED WIFE

Of course, not all sightings are dramatic and distressing – sometimes they are quiet and reassuring.

An elderly Worcestershire widower, who had lost his wife in the winter of 2000, engaged two cleaning ladies to manage his home. He was in the habit of retiring to his study to get some peace while they went about their chores. One day, the elder of the two interrupted him to ask if she needed to make up a bed for his visitor. As there was no one else staying in the house he thought the cleaners were joking. But when the younger one insisted she had seen a woman in one of the downstairs rooms, he went with them to check but they found the room empty. The only exit to the house was by the front door, which was fitted with a scraper that would have made a grating noise if someone had left that way. As the widower's study overlooked the drive, he would also have witnessed any comings and goings. The widower asked the younger woman to describe the woman in her vision. She told him the ghost had had shoulder-length brown hair and was wearing a rose-coloured cardigan. The man's wife had worn a cardigan of that colour; her hair was grey, but in her younger years it had been brown. Then the young woman mentioned seeing a photograph of the lady in an upstairs room; she said the widower was also in the picture. It was a photograph of the couple in their younger years.

THE RELATIVES WHO
STAY BEHIND

If you aren't expecting a visit from the dear departed, it is a shock when they reappear!

In the late 1980s a young couple were staying at a guest house in Caerleon, near Newport, in South Wales, when the wife noticed a face peering down at them from a corner of the ceiling. It was the face of an old man, illuminated in an unnatural way. Her husband saw it too and stretched out his hand as if to touch it, at which point his wife screamed and hid under the bedclothes. She later realized that the apparition was her grandfather, who had recently died. She had been his favourite grandchild. When she grew calmer, she reassured herself with the thought that he was probably just checking to see if she was all right.

Vianne Roberts lost her grandparents in the 1980s. One summer's day she was sitting in her flat when she saw her grandmother walk across the hallway just 60 cm (2 ft) from where she was sitting. The old woman was smiling and as solid as she would have been in life. She was so solid, in fact, that Vianne felt she could have reached out and touched her grandmother's ghost if she had had the presence of mind to do so before the vision vanished. A few months later, Vianne saw her grandfather sitting in a chair by the living-room door. She saw him on more than one occasion, but only when she looked at the TV, which was switched off. Whenever she looked directly at the chair, her grandfather disappeared!

In a book entitled *Haunted Holidays* by Anne Bradford and David Taylor, another young man, identified only as Peter, had a life-changing encounter in 1987 while staying with a religious youth group in Northfield, near Birmingham, UK. He went to the bathroom and encountered an elderly man dressed in old-fashioned working clothes – scarf, jacket and trousers. The old man glared at him and Peter left hurriedly. When he told his hostess what he had seen, she didn't seem surprised – she said that Peter had met her late husband. Peter had strong religious convictions at the time and didn't believe in ghosts, but the experience prompted him to abandon his religion.

A HANGING

A woman who wishes to be known only as Jenny offered to make curtains for a friend and hang them for her. The friend had just bought an old cottage which was rumoured to have been the home of the notorious Judge Jeffreys, 'the hanging judge'. Jeffreys presided over the 'Bloody Assizes' in late 17th-century Britain, in which about three hundred rebels against the rule of

King James II were sentenced to death. Jenny arrived at the empty cottage on an August evening and began to hang the upstairs bedroom curtains. As she turned her back to the window, she felt something pulling her backwards. She swung round to see the figure of a tall man, aged about thirty, of medium build and with long hair. He was standing in shadow, so she couldn't tell if he was dressed in black or if the shadows made his clothes appear dark. At first she thought it must be her husband playing a prank, but then she remembered he was elsewhere at the time. A moment later, the figure vanished in front of her eyes.

When Jenny mentioned the incident, her friend told her that Judge Jeffreys was said to have sat at that very window to watch the hangings of his victims. Intrigued, Jenny looked out a book on the period and found that a portrait of Jeffreys corresponded to the vision of the man she had seen, except that he had appeared to her as a younger man.

PAST IMPRESSIONS

When Robin Gibb of the Bee Gees was a small boy, his family lived in an old house in Oxfordshire which had once been a seminary for Roman Catholic priests. The young Robin often told his mother that he could see the former inhabitants of the house walking in and out as they had done a century or more ago. His mother was able to confirm the mode of dress and other details her son described; she also discovered that the family he talked of and named as John and Mary and their friend Elizabeth had indeed lived there. Robin also described a little boy who he referred to as 'never having grown up'; his description corresponded to that of a child of the family who had died in infancy.

SIBLING SUPPORT

The deceased often appear as radiant apparitions, even if they died violently or suffered a debilitating illness at the end of life. Some manifest as they were in younger, happier years, suggesting that the image they project conforms to their ideal of themselves. But the next story suggests that perhaps those who die young continue to age 'on the other side'.

In the early 1970s, Lynn Bovis's mother had just given birth to a son and was lying in bed giving thanks for a safe delivery as the infant slept in his cot. The room was illuminated by the full moon, so the mother was certain that what she saw next was not a trick of the light. Two female apparitions appeared in the room next to the cot. One was slightly older than the other and both were wearing long gowns and 'shone like a candle flame'. The younger one remained by the cot, smiling at the baby, while the older woman sat on the bed and put her hand on Lynn's mother's hand, but the mother pulled away. The two figures then vanished. The only explanation Lynn's mother was able to give her children when they grew up was that she had lost two sisters when they were babies and perhaps they were returning to make sure that their sister and her child were all right.

TWO HANDS TO HOLD YOU

It seems that the personalities of deceased people may also change after they have crossed over. When Chris Jones was a young man of twenty, he was seized by two phantom hands which emerged from the back of the sofa he was sitting on and gave him a gentle squeeze. He had frozen just moments before, as if sensing an otherworldly presence. Although he tried to struggle when he felt the hands take hold of him, he stopped as soon as he sensed an overwhelming feeling of contentment and reassurance. Instinctively he 'knew' that the hug had come from his paternal grandfather who had died some years earlier, although the old man had never held his grandson during his lifetime and was described as withdrawn and undemonstrative.

COLLEGE GHOST

In 1905, an undergraduate at Cambridge University reported seeing a ghost in the old lodge of Corpus Christi college during the Easter break. One afternoon, the student was at work in his rooms when he became conscious of a curious and apparently causeless sense of unease. Getting up and looking out of the window, he saw a man with long hair leaning out of an upper window in the opposite set of rooms. Only the man's head and shoulders were visible and he remained very still, seeming to fix the undergraduate with a long, hostile stare. When the young man went to investigate, he found the door to the room was locked.

The ghost is believed to be Dr Butts, Master of the College from 1626 to 1632, who described himself as a 'destitute and forsaken man'. Butts was found hanging by his garters in the rooms on Easter Sunday 1632 and has haunted the college ever since.

Ghosts of the Great Outdoors

Ghosts are traditionally associated with dilapidated old houses and crumbling ruins, but it seems that some phantoms don't like to be confined to draughty castle corridors and gloomy old houses. They prefer the great outdoors, where they can wander at will and spook unsuspecting hikers.

In Mammoth Cave, Kentucky, tour guides and geologists have encountered the ghost of former slave Stephen Bishop, who a hundred years earlier mapped the 'grand, gloomy and peculiar place' he loved so much. He even turned down the chance to earn his freedom because it would have meant leaving the caves.

In the 1990s, science teacher Larry Purcell left his tour group for a couple of minutes and found himself facing a black man and woman and their two children, all dressed in 19th-century clothes. Purcell moved aside to let them pass, but as he did so he realized that he had just seen the ghosts of Stephen Bishop and his family. Purcell wasn't the only person to see the former slave, but many of those who claim to have seen Bishop, wearing his white trousers, dark shirt and white waistcoat, assumed he was a tour guide in period costume.

Another tour guide, Gary Bremer, was boating with

four companions on Echo river, an underground stream inside the caves, when they heard a woman calling. There was no one else in the caves at the time apart from the five men. It was then that Bremer recalled the story of Melissa who in the 1850s had lured her lover to his death in the caves. Intending to teach him a lesson for spurning her affections, Melissa enticed him into the underground labyrinth and left him to find his way out. But she felt guilty and returned to rescue him. Alas, he was lost, never to be found again, and Melissa wandered aimlessly, calling his name in vain. A few years later she died of consumption, but her ghost is said to haunt the caves, searching for her dead lover.

THE FARMER WHO PLOUGHED BY MOONLIGHT

Back in 1892, the *Chicago Tribune* ran a story about a Florida farmer who saw a previous tenant ploughing his field by moonlight. Curiously, the farmer could see the ploughman and his oxen as if by daylight, yet the surrounding hills were in comparative darkness. When the farmer asked his eldest son to talk to the ploughman the boy did as he was told, but returned saying he couldn't see anyone in the field. 'But you just walked right through him!' said his father.

Determined to confront the phantom, the farmer went out into the field but could see no one. He then returned to the house and looked back to see the ploughman still at work, his features concealed under a broad-brimmed hat, his whip soundlessly snaking over the oxen.

The *Tribune* reported that the farmer was so shaken by this vision he invited his neighbours to witness the apparition. They too went out into the field but saw nothing, though they had been able to see the ploughman and his team from the house.

SPECTRAL SOLDIERS

Stories and sightings of spectral soldiers and phantom armies are not uncommon. As well as ghosts from the distant past, the following stories suggest that more recent conflicts have their share of unquiet spirits.

THE SAD-EYED SERGEANT

After the First World War, people's interest in Spiritualism intensified as many grieving families consulted mediums in an attempt to contact their menfolk who had been killed or declared missing in action. Interest in the occult grew, even though this meant incurring the disapproval of the Church.

A number of personal accounts of ghostly encounters were published and instantly became bestsellers. *Dreams and Visions of the War* by Rosa Stuart (1917) included the following account of a British wife's 'vision' of her soldier husband.

On the evening of 25 September 1915, the wife of a soldier serving in France with the Devon Regiment was sitting on her bed in a room in Bournemouth. She was sharing the room with another woman and they were discussing the war and other matters. They were generally in a contented frame of mind, as that morning the other woman had received a letter from her husband telling her that he was safe and well. Suddenly the young wife broke off in mid-sentence and stared into space. There, standing before her, dressed in his sergeant's uniform, was her husband.

For two or three minutes she sat looking at him, struck by the expression of sadness in his eyes. Getting up quickly, she approached the spot where he was standing, but by the time she reached it he had disappeared. She felt sure that the vision had foretold his death. Soon afterwards, she received a letter from the War Office informing her that her husband had been killed at the Battle of Loos on the very day that she had seen him standing beside her bed.

The Ghostly Cavalry of Le Cateau

The best-known ghost story of the Great War is the 'Angel of Mons', based on a tale by British journalist Arthur Machen, who later admitted it was a work of fiction used to boost morale. He couldn't have foreseen that his piece would encourage soldiers who had been serving at the Front to share their personal stories of phantom armies.

Responding to Mr Machen in the *London Evening News* on 14 September, 1915, a British officer described what he and his men had seen at Le Cateau on 27 August, 1914.

'On the night of the 27th I was riding along in the column with two other officers. We had been talking and doing our best to keep from falling asleep on our horses.

'As we rode along I became conscious of the fact that, in the fields on both sides of the road along which we were marching, I could see a very large body of horsemen. These horsemen had the appearance of squadrons of cavalry, and they seemed to be riding across the fields and going in the same direction as we were going, and keeping level with us.

'The night was not very dark, and I fancied that I could see the squadron of these cavalrymen quite distinctly. I did not say a word about it at first, but I watched them for about twenty minutes. The other two officers had stopped talking.

'At last one of them asked me if I saw anything in the fields. I then told him what I had seen. The third officer then confessed that he, too, had been watching these horsemen for the past twenty minutes.

'So convinced were we that they were really cavalry that, at the next halt, one of the officers took a party of men out to reconnoitre, and found no one there. The night then grew darker, and we saw no more.

'The same phenomenon was seen by many men in our column. Of course, we were all dog-tired and overtaxed, but it is an extraordinary thing that the same phenomenon should be witnessed by so many people.

'I myself am absolutely convinced that I saw these horsemen; and I feel sure that they did not exist only in my imagination. I do not attempt to explain the mystery, I only state facts.'

PATTON'S PHANTOMS

Although General George S. Patton was a down-to-earth soldier, he had several paranormal experiences which convinced him that the dead can assist the living in times of crisis. During the Battle of the Argonne in the First World War, as Patton was pinned down by machine-gun fire, he saw the ghostly disembodied faces of his grandfather and great uncles glaring at him with disapproval. Spurred into action by this vision, the future US general rallied his men and made a daring frontal assault against the German trenches, for which he was later awarded the Distinguished Service Cross.

During the Second World War, Patton said he was visited several times in his tent by the spirit of his father, who had died in 1927. Patton said the apparition eased his anxiety and he found the encounter so real it was as if he was talking to the old man in his study back home.

THE PADDY FIELD PHANTOMS

In the spring of 1993, almost two decades after the end of the Vietnam War, a local farmer was walking to his paddy field in the early morning when he saw the spirits of his dead wife and children where their house had once stood. It had been burned to the ground in 1968 during a massacre in which his family had been killed. The wife was sitting on a stone with her children standing behind her; the children appeared afraid that their parents would argue, as they used to do. The woman was scowling, but she said nothing. She didn't need to – her appearance at that moment made it clear to her husband it was time to give his family a decent burial. To do this he would need to disinter them from their shallow grave and lay them to rest in a proper plot. But he had no money. Fortunately, that same day a member of his wife's family came to visit with her wealthy husband and they offered to pay for the reburial. The woman had decided to travel to the village after being visited by the spirit of the dead wife and her children in her dreams.

In an unrelated incident, three tourists holidaying in the Phuoc Tuy province of Vietnam claim to have seen a phantom soldier. He was bleeding from a wound in his neck and groaning in an English or Australian accent, 'I need help, where am I?' Then he walked away from them and vanished into the undergrowth.

THE GUARD WHO WASN'T THERE

The Second Gulf War of 2003 was brief, but it saw many acts of brutality and sudden violent death on both sides, including the deaths of innocent civilians. All combatants were in a heightened state of alert and under severe stress for hours or even days, so it's not surprising that some of them experienced events they cannot explain. And, while the peculiar desert environment is known to exert a strange disorientating effect on the mind, it cannot explain away what happened to a US soldier who posted the following story under the pen name Kanika. He was deployed with a mobile medical unit among a cluster of abandoned buildings in a vast, featureless stretch of sand far from the nearest village. He claims that several soldiers experienced 'strange phenomena' in the area.

At 2am, Kanika and his companion were on guard duty when the phone rang. Naturally, they assumed it would be someone calling to report a medical emergency. However, instead of an American voice on the other end of the line, Kanika heard a babble of people speaking in Arabic. The sounds were muffled, but there was no mistaking the panic in the voices. Assuming that the caller(s) had dialled the wrong number, Kanika hung up, but recorded it in the log all the same. At 8am, Kanika and his buddy went off-duty and handed over the log to their replacements. But when Kanika mentioned the phone call, the relief team looked at him as though he was mad. They pointed to the lead behind the telephone table – it wasn't plugged in.

A Mr Muniz posted the following personal story on a paranormal activity website in response to a request for true ghost stories.

The Second Gulf War had been over for several weeks when Mr Muniz's platoon was ordered to occupy an Iraqi airforce base close to a large ammunition dump. Their task was to guard it against attack by insurgents, so one night Muniz and a fellow NCO volunteered to take a shift. They were armed with automatic rifles and both had night-vision goggles that could pick out anything moving in the dark up to several hundred metres away. It was eerily quiet; all that Muniz and his comrade could hear was the sound of approaching footsteps. Flipping the safety catch on their weapons, they scanned the perimeter through the goggles, but couldn't see anything. The footsteps came closer, a distinct clip of boots on the approach road. There could be no mistake – someone was walking down the road towards them, but there was nothing to be seen, either with the naked eye or through the night-vision goggles.

Then, just as the footsteps reached the perimeter fence, they stopped, turned and retreated. By this time, Muniz's companion was on his feet and standing by the road. He heard the footsteps walk right up to him, then turn and go back the way they had come. This occurred three times, until both soldiers realized what they were hearing. It was the sound of a sentry pacing back and forth on guard duty. But there wasn't another living soul in sight.

The next night, their replacements heard the very same thing. They opened fire, but failed to find a body.

5

MANY
HAPPY
RETURNS

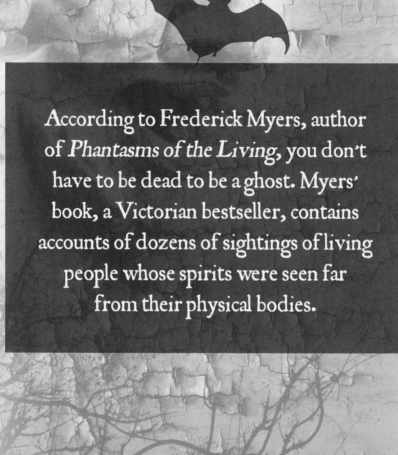

According to Frederick Myers, author of *Phantasms of the Living*, you don't have to be dead to be a ghost. Myers' book, a Victorian bestseller, contains accounts of dozens of sightings of living people whose spirits were seen far from their physical bodies.

THIS phenomenon is known as an out-of-body experience (OBE) and usually occurs when the individual is in the deepest stages of sleep. However, it can be induced by illness, a sudden, life-threatening shock, or an emotional crisis that causes a temporary detachment of the spirit 'double' from the physical body. People who are fully conscious while experiencing this detachment find it a profoundly liberating, invigorating, life-changing event that alters their perception of reality.

Many people, for whatever reason, dismiss OBEs as dreams; but there have been cases where a witness has seen a dead person's spirit when his or her physical body is known to be elsewhere. Margaret was eleven years old and living in Leeds, UK, when she and a number of friends saw what they thought was an angel in the night sky. It emerged from behind the roof of one of the houses, was 'silver and shimmering' and appeared to have a silver cord trailing behind it as it rose higher in the sky. The friends later learnt that their sighting of the 'angel' had coincided with the death of a woman in the house that night.

THE MOMENT OF DEATH

What is it like to die? This question has been answered by the many thousands of people around the world who claim to have had an out-of-body or near-death experience. For those who can recall floating free of their physical bodies, it is more than a vivid dream. It offers personal, irrefutable proof that we are more than physical beings. We have a spirit double (the astral soul referred to in Hindu and Tibetan traditions) that can be released naturally and spontaneously when we are in a deep state of relaxation, most commonly during sleep, or during a life-threatening crisis when the trauma triggers a temporary separation of mind and body. According to many cultures and traditions around the world, mind and spirit are one and the same and the physical shell we inhabit is merely a covering we discard at the moment of death.

This explains why many ghosts of the recently deceased return with reassurance or warnings for the loved ones they leave behind. By contrast, ghosts from an earlier time do not tend to interact with the living because they are merely echoes in the atmosphere or vibrations infused into the fabric of a building.

Although OBEs were recorded in ancient times and are referred to in the Bible (St Paul's ascent to the seventh heaven 'in the spirit' and Jesus' manifestation after the Crucifixion are just two of many examples), it was not until the 19th century that this phenomenon was considered universal and worthy of serious study.

IN PERIL IN THE ALPS

One of the first Europeans to conduct such a study was Professor Albert Helm, a Swiss geologist and avid mountain climber, whose own brush with death encouraged him to seek out others who had shared a similar experience.

In 1871, Professor Helm was climbing in the Alps when he lost his footing and plunged to what he thought would be certain death.

'I had the feeling of submission to necessity. Then I saw arching over me – my eyes were directed upwards – a beautiful blue heaven with small violet and rosy-red clouds… I felt myself go softly backwards into this magnificent heaven – without anxiety, without grief. It was a great, glorious moment!'

Miraculously, Professor Helm survived the fall and, by 1892, had accumulated sufficient anecdotal evidence to justify publishing his first article on the subject of near-death experience. He identified several significant common elements in every account he was given: namely, the sense of existing in a moment beyond time; the life review unfolding as if one was a spectator of one's own life; and the blissful all-enveloping peace in place of the terror one would have expected.

That same year, two British researchers, William James and Richard Hodgson, published their findings in the *Journal of Psychical Research*. They included an account given by the Reverend Bertrand, who had become separated from his friends while climbing in the Alps and had been overtaken by the certainty that he was freezing to death.

He felt himself becoming detached from his body and, as he floated free, he noticed that he was connected to his petrified body by what he described as an 'elastic string'. Free from cold and pain, he rose into the air 'like a balloon' and observed with irritation his fellow climbers who were now taking the right-hand path to the summit, against his explicit instructions. He also saw the guide taking a drink and food from the provisions the Reverend had given him to carry.

As the Reverend became acclimatized to floating in his new 'subtle body', he decided to explore, drifting over to the hotel where he saw his wife alight from a carriage with four companions and enter the lobby. At this point he had no physical sensations whatever, only a mild regret that he could not sever the cord that bound him to the frozen body he could see below and be free. However, in the next instant he was jerked violently back into his body, as the guide attempted to restore his circulation.

'I had a hope – the balloon seemed much too big for the mouth. Suddenly I uttered an awful roar like a wild beast; the corpse swallowed the balloon, and Bertrand was Bertrand again.'

And indeed he was, for the first thing he did was admonish the guide for taking the rest of the party by the more precarious route and for stealing his food and drink. As for his wife, she was relieved to hear that her husband had been revived, but at a loss as to how he knew she had changed her plans to make a detour to the hotel with her four friends.

PHANTOM FORERUNNERS

The phenomenon known as a 'phantom forerunner' is more difficult to explain, other than to say it appears that some people are able to project an image of themselves unconsciously to another location merely by visualizing a journey they intend to make. But even this does not explain how it is that others have seen them arrive 'in spirit', dressed in clothes they would not be wearing until the day of their journey!

In 1995, a British woman visited her retired sister in Swansea, South Wales. She knew many of her older sister's neighbours by sight and was concerned to hear that one of them was terminally ill and unlikely to leave hospital. She was therefore surprised to hear her sister remark that she had seen the patient walk up the steps to her flat. Her sister said the woman must have walked some distance, because there was no car in sight and none had been heard pulling up or driving away. But surely a terminally ill woman would not have been discharged from hospital? Even if she had, wouldn't she have been brought home by ambulance and delivered safely inside by paramedics?

So the younger sister went to the window. She, too, saw the sick woman outside her apartment and noted what she was wearing – a long navy blue coat. The older sister commented that the sick woman's hair had evidently not been brushed, which was unlike her as she was fastidious about her appearance. The older sister mentioned this strange occurrence to a neighbour who had also seen the sick woman and remembered that she had looked smart in her long navy coat, but that her hair had been unkempt.

Some time later, the sisters heard that the patient had not been discharged from hospital; but at the exact moment at which they had seen her outside she had sat up in bed and demanded to go home. She was finally allowed out for a few days to set her affairs in order. She was then seen again by her neighbours, arriving at her apartment dressed in the same long, navy blue coat worn by her 'ghost' some days earlier.

BILOCATION

Living apparitions involve the projection of the etheric body (or spirit 'double') to another location. They can occur when the individual is either in a deep state of relaxation or has been temporarily separated from his or her physical body because of a life-threatening condition, as with a 'crisis apparition'.

However, it seems that some rare individuals can project their etheric double to another location at will, through conscious effort and concentration. These people have appeared at their chosen location in so solid a form as to give the impression that they are there in the flesh.

One of the most remarkable examples of this phenomenon was recorded by the 17th-century Roman Catholic missionary, Father Alonso de Benavides. When Father Alonso arrived at Isolita in New Mexico in 1622 he discovered that the Jumano Indians had already been converted to Catholicism, although no missionaries had been sent by his or any other order. It is believed that

Father Alonso was the first Spanish-speaking person to encounter the indigenous people of this region, but there was no denying the fact that the Jumano knew the liturgy in their own tongue and had altars and crosses that would have been impossible to construct without the aid of a representative of the Catholic Church.

The Indians informed Father Alonso that they had been converted by a beautiful young woman in blue, who had been among them for several years and instructed them in the necessary rituals in their native tongue. She had predicted that other white missionaries would follow and advised the Jumano to make these newcomers welcome. Then she had disappeared. The nuns of the Poor Clare order wore blue habits, so Father Alonso assumed they must have sent the anonymous missionary. Then he remembered that they were a strictly cloistered order and initiates were not allowed to leave the sanctuary of the convent.

However, Father Alonso would not let the matter rest; eventually his investigations led him to Ágreda, in Spain, where he heard a strange confession from Sister Mary of Jesus, Mother Superior of the Ágreda convent. She admitted that she had converted the Jumano, but had done so without leaving the convent. She had travelled 'in spirit' during a light trance. Later on she would recall a dream in which she had journeyed to an exotic land where she had taught the gospel. Father Alonso was sceptical at first, but Sister Mary provided him with a description of the region together with details of the clothing and customs of its inhabitants. She couldn't have gleaned this information from books or as a traveller, because the tribe had only just been discovered by the outside world. As for overcoming the language barrier, she had no explanation for this other than to say she had simply spoken to the Jumano from her heart, and God had translated for her.

DEATHBED VISIONS

A deathbed confession is considered to be an indisputable statement of fact in the eyes of the law. So it is with a deathbed vision, for at the moment of death it is assumed that a person wants his or her conscience to be clear. This was the reasoning behind a series of scientific studies into the phenomenon conducted at the end of the 19th century, when public interest in Spiritualism was at its height. While mediums astounded clients with materializations, voluminous amounts of ectoplasm and noisy table rappings, some members of the scientific community focused on recording the last words of the dying in an attempt to establish some kind of understanding of the afterlife.

In January 1924 Lady Florence Barrett, an

obstetrician, was called to the bedside of a woman who was expected to die in childbirth. As the poor woman lay there, drawing her last breath, she stared into the corner of the room, smiled broadly and said, 'Lovely brightness – wonderful beings.' Then she cried out, 'Why, it's Father! Oh, he's so glad I'm coming; he is so glad!'

She lived just long enough to hold her baby, then exclaimed 'I can't stay. I am coming!' Lady Barrett saw nothing, but the dying woman was evidently referring to an unseen presence when she said, 'He has Vida with him.' It was only after the woman had lost her fight for life that Lady Barrett learnt that Vida was the patient's sister. Vida had died three weeks earlier, but this news had been kept from the mother-to-be for fear of the shock it might cause her in her fragile state of health.

Lady Barrett was so impressed by this experience that she persuaded her husband, the eminent Irish physicist Sir William Barrett, to undertake a serious study of the deathbed phenomenon.

Sir William's conclusions were published in 1926, under the title *Deathbed Visions*, but his colleagues were convinced that he had merely recorded a succession of hallucinations. In defence of the book, Sir William argued that all his subjects had been lucid at the time of death. Furthermore, he said they had exhibited signs of genuine surprise at what they described; and their descriptions often contradicted what they had been conditioned to expect by their religious upbringing.

AT THE HOUR OF DEATH

Three decades later, New York parapsychologist Karlis Osis conducted his own comprehensive study and concluded that deathbed visions were not influenced by drugs or the patient's symptoms. Moreover, only the terminally ill had described seeing loved ones who had passed over. Mentally ill patients did not claim to see such things, which they may have been expected to had the visions been hallucinations. Religious beliefs and expectations of what might be seen at the point of death also appeared to have no bearing on what was described, which also suggested that the deathbed visions were genuine.

Encouraged by his findings, Osis embarked on a joint study with Icelandic psychologist Erlendur Haraldsson. During the 1970s they interviewed 1,708 patients in America and India. Their findings, published in 1977 under the title *At the Hour of Death*, included the following examples.

A paramedic who sat at the bedside of an elderly man later reported that the patient's chest pains subsided whenever he spoke of his vision. 'It was so beautiful, you just can't tell anyone,' he told the paramedic. 'It was a breathtaking scene, more so than anything in life.'

The same effect was seen in an elderly woman who had been described by her nurse as very unpleasant prior to these visions.

'One night she called me to see how bright and lovely heaven is,' said the nurse. 'Then she looked at me and seemed surprised: "Oh, but you can't see it, you aren't here [in heaven], you are over there." She became very peaceful and happy… and she permitted her meanness to die… I don't think these are hallucinations, they are… very real.'

It is revealing that while the attendant medical staff and family members don't share the visions, they are nevertheless impressed by the sense of peace that overwhelms the patient and some speak of sensing a change in the atmosphere in the room. Wilma Ashby made a miraculous recovery after being visited by her dead twin brother Willard, leading her husband to remark that he felt as though he had been struck by lightning when he entered her hospital room. Speaking of another terminally ill patient, a nurse noted that the woman was 'transformed' by the presence of an unseen person. 'Her attitude seemed to have changed entirely. This was more than [just] a change of the [depressed] mood I had seen her in many times before… It seemed as if there was something [here that was] just a little beyond us...There was something which made us feel that... she [had] some contact with the beyond and it had a happy effect on her.'

Osis and Haraldsson were convinced that such cases 'seem to support the hypothesis that deathbed visions are, in part, based on extrasensory perception of some form of external reality rather than having entirely subjective origins'.

RECENT RESEARCH

More recently, British neuropsychiatrist Dr Peter Fenwick, president of the British branch of the International Association for Near-Death Studies, published a comprehensive survey of the phenomenon, including the following account.

In the 1980s, the nephew of a man who had survived the horrors of the Somme, for which he was awarded the Military Cross, was sitting with his dying uncle when the frail old man suddenly sat up and looked across the room. He became very animated and was talking to people that neither his nephew nor his elderly wife could see. He addressed each of these people by name and appeared very happy to see them again. It became evident that they were men he had known during the early days of the Great War, but they had been killed in the battle. He had commanded a unit that had suffered many casualties and only three of his men had survived. In his excitement he seemed to forget his pain and a 'look of wonderment' illuminated his face. The nephew told Dr Fenwick, 'I will never forget that night and though I could not see his friends, I have no doubt whatsoever that they were there.' His uncle died a couple of days later.

FAMILY VISIT

One of the few deathbed visions experienced by someone who subsequently recovered was posted by Nancy on the Paranormalia website in February 2009.

Nancy had been hospitalized with a high fever. While slipping in and out of consciousness, she recalled seeing deceased members of her family and also friends who had passed over standing in the corner of her hospital room. Then her late grandfather sat on the bed and she was overcome by a feeling of perfect peace. She was euphoric and not just because he reassured her that everything would be all right. She didn't know at the time whether this meant she would recover, despite the doctor's prognosis, or die and find herself in a tranquil afterlife state. All she knew for certain was that the sense of wellbeing washed away all anxiety. When she returned to waking consciousness, a nurse asked who she had been talking to. Nancy was surprised to learn that she had been alone the entire time. She then went to sleep. When she awoke the next morning, her fever had broken. Three months later, she made a complete recovery.

AFTER-DEATH COMMUNICATIONS

The earliest account of an after-death communication conveyed in a dream is thought to have been recorded by Marcus Tullius Cicero in the first century BCE. It describes two travellers, who separated on reaching the city of Megara. One accepted an invitation to stay at the house of a friend while his companion took a room at an inn. During the night, the first traveller dreamt that his companion came to him and said the innkeeper had murdered him. His body had been thrown into a cart and covered with dung. The innkeeper planned to dispose of the body outside the city, but if the cart could be stopped at the city gates the crime would be uncovered and the guilty man punished. Convinced by his vision, the first traveller woke at dawn and went to the city gates, where he stopped the cart and uncovered the corpse, exactly as the ghost of his dead friend had requested.

Author Emma Heathcote-James has made a comprehensive study of after-death communications (a term coined in the 1990s by Bill and Judy Guggenheim, authors of *Hello From Heaven*). Her book, entitled *After-Death Communication*, includes deathbed visions, vivid dreams of meetings with the deceased, auditory messages, phantom phone calls, apparitions and even physical contact.

Some witnesses were startled by their experiences, because they were unexpected or contradicted their religious beliefs, but the majority were oddly reassured. Karen Browne's testimonial is a good example. She was living with her parents and younger brother in a first-floor flat. Her maternal grandparents lived in an apartment on the ground floor. One morning Karen awoke from a deep sleep to see her grandfather standing at the foot of her bed. Smiling, he said calmly, 'I'm going away now, my wee dove.' Reassured by his apparent contentment and his use of her familiar pet name, Karen thought no more of it and went back to sleep. Before she did so, she glanced at the clock – it was six in the morning and she didn't have to get up for work for another hour. Moments later, she was woken by the ringing of the phone and a cry from her mother downstairs. Her grandmother was calling to say that Karen's grandfather had just died.

Karen describes feeling strangely calm as she dealt with the practicalities of calling the family physician and the undertakers and caring for the grieving relatives who came to view the body laid out in a coffin in the bedroom. When Karen went to view the body herself, she remembered what she had seen earlier that morning and knew that her grandfather had come to say goodbye at the moment of his death. She was reassured that the body in the coffin was just an empty shell.

BIG JOHN

In the late 1920s, in West Pittsfield, Massachusetts, a young boy befriended a dark-skinned Ukranian man, Big John Rinko. John worked at the icehouse, packing slabs of ice on to railroad cars. During their lunch break, he would share his sandwiches of dark bread and spiced meat with the boy, whom he nicknamed 'little onion'. In 1932, Big John died at the age of forty-five. This upset the boy greatly and made him think about life and what it might be like when it was his parents' turn to go.

A month or so later, the boy was playing with his brother behind an empty bunkhouse (the icemen having left at the close of the season) when he saw the smiling face of Big John at a window. John was dressed in his heavy check shirt and greasy wool cap. He beckoned and the boy ran to him, calling out his name. Just then, his brother called, 'But he's dead!' As Big John strode towards his little friend, the boy realized that this was true and the ghost vanished. A moment later, the brother entered the bunkhouse; although no one was there, the air was heavy with the unmistakable aroma of spiced sandwiches, tobacco and sweaty wool. When the boy returned to the bunkhouse with his dog, the animal howled pitifully as it never had done before, as if sensing someone was there with them.

A GLIMPSE OF HEAVEN

The following experience was related by a bereaved mother and is not as rare as one might imagine, although those who are privileged to share such a 'vision' find it profoundly personal and unforgettable.

One year after her four-year-old son, Toby, had died from a brain haemorrhage, a young nurse had an exceptionally vivid dream – she was standing on a riverbank and her son was watching her from the far side. His side of the river was a paradise, with beautiful trees, singing birds and lush grass and flowers. Toby looked exactly the same as he had on the day he died. But, although he was clearly happy, he was also concerned that his mother was trying to cross the river before her time. She later described his manner as that of an adult and hers as that of an overeager child who was being restrained for her own good. Toby was the older, wiser soul, patiently reassuring her that he was at peace and where he belonged. When she awoke from her dream, the nurse was deeply disappointed it was over; yet she was comforted because she sensed that it had been real, as real as anything experienced in the physical world.

NO FEAR OF DEATH

Agnes O'Reilly had a similar dream, only hers continued after she had woken up. Agnes' mother died in September 1982, leaving her daughter grieving and troubled as she was aware that her mother had feared death. Six weeks later, Agnes' mother came to her in a dream and explained in considerable detail how she had died. She said she hadn't realized what was happening to her until she had seen her own mother and father and her sister Mary who had died many years earlier. Agnes then woke to see her mother standing at the foot of her bed. She was dressed in white and hovering with her feet a few centimetres from the floor. She assured Agnes that she was happy now and gave her a big smile. When Agnes asked her sister, who had been present at their mother's death, for the details, the sister described them just as her mother had said.

EARLY INTO THE WORLD

When Nancy Denofio was born prematurely in September 1949, doctors gave her only days to live. She was so tiny that she could fit in the palm of her mother's hand. No child weighing so little had survived, but her mother would not give up hope – and it wasn't stubbornness or religious faith that gave her courage.

One morning, depressed and anxious as she sat in her hospital bed, Nancy's mother saw two men at the end of it. One was her father, who had died two years earlier, and the other was her father-in-law, who was also 'in spirit'. She had never met him, but recognized his face from photographs. Her father told her not to worry or listen to the doctors; he said the baby would survive and grow up to be a healthy child. The medical staff at the hospital found the mother's positive outlook worrying. One of them told her she should pray for her baby's merciful death because, if by a miracle she should live, she would have a lifetime of serious health problems. Three months later, on Christmas Day 1949, mother and daughter left hospital happy and healthy.

UNEXPECTED APPENDECTOMY

Dreams can also relay warnings from loved ones on the other side. British dental student Steve Cowling was just eighteen years old when he was diagnosed with a deformed gall bladder that needed to be operated on. The night before the operation, he had a vivid dream in which his recently deceased father appeared and told him that he should have his appendix removed as well. The warning was both timely and accurate. The surgeon who performed the operation did as Steve requested and confirmed that the appendix would have caused trouble if it hadn't been taken out at that time. It is significant that both Agnes and Steve shared a strikingly similar vision of the pastoral paradise in which they met their departed loved ones. Steve's father also told him he had to remain where he was, and that it was not his time to cross over.

PREDICTION OF DEATH

Author Emma Heathcote-James describes the following account by the daughter of a woman who had to make a difficult decision to return to this world.

The woman had awoken one night to find herself floating above her body, which was lying motionless in bed. She sensed there was another presence hovering above her, someone she knew but couldn't name. Great love emanated from this person and the woman felt an urge to be with him or her, but she couldn't rise any higher. Then she heard the person say, 'If you come any higher you will leave your body and never return. You have a choice. You can come with us now, or you can stay here with your family, but staying means that you will suffer two years of pain and illness before you can join us again.'

The mother made an effort of will to visit her sleeping children in their rooms. As she looked down on them, she knew she could not leave them. When she woke, she told her husband of her experience. Two months later, she was diagnosed with terminal cancer. She died exactly two years to the day after making that fateful choice.

PHONE CALLS FROM THE DEAD

The phone rings. You answer it, but there is no one at the other end. Dead silence. We've all received these calls and there is no mystery behind many of them – automatic random dialling by marketing and other cold-calling companies is routine and commonplace, one of the hazards of modern life. But not every cold call comes from the living.

A female friend told paranormal researcher Jim Hale that she had received a call in the middle of the night from her father, who said he was phoning to check that she was all right. Then he hung up. There was no mistaking the voice – she recognized it immediately – yet her father had passed away several years earlier.

This phenomenon is not as rare as one might imagine. There have been so many recorded cases that, in 1979, parapsychologists D. Scott Rogo and Raymond Bayless compiled what they claimed to be the first book on the subject (although *Voices From Beyond by Telephone* by Carlos G. Ramos, using the pen-name Oscar D'Argonell, had already been published in 1925). In *Phone Calls From the Dead*, Rogo and Bayless tried in each instance to obtain verification of phantom interference from more than one individual. On several occasions, the person taking the call passed the phone to another person, who confirmed the identity of the caller. In one case, two people sharing the same phone number (but using different phones) held a long conversation with the phantom caller and later confirmed they had both heard the same voice on the end of the line. Sceptics would argue that these calls were made by heartless pranksters, but a number of inexplicable examples refute this theory.

VOICES ON THE LINE

One Christmas Eve, Bonnie O. went to bed early, only to be woken by a phone call from a woman she identified as her mother, who had died three years earlier. There was static on the line and the voice cut in and out, but there was no mistaking the caller as Bonnie's mother had had a strong Norwegian accent.

In 1995, Mrs Wilson of Ellesmere Port in Liverpool rang her local radio station hoping to put a question to psychic James Byrne on the evening talk show. The lines were jammed with callers, but at ten that evening after the show had finished Mrs Wilson received a phone call from an elderly man who identified himself as her late grandfather. He told her he was fine and that he was with her grandmother and other 'nice people who had passed over'. He spoke reassuringly as he had always done, insisting that she should not dwell in the past but move on. His last wish was for her to pass on his love to her children.

She was sure the voice was that of her grandfather, but she checked the call record anyway. The automated voice told her that the last call had been made from her own number. As there was no extension in the house, she could only assume she had taken a call from the other side.

IMPORTANT INFORMATION

Rogo and Bayless identified several varieties of phantom calls. The most common they categorized as 'simple'. This describes a very brief call that does not involve a two-way conversation. It consists of a short message to reassure the recipient or convey some important information. The second type of call, categorized as 'prolonged', typically occurs when the recipient isn't aware that the caller is deceased. A third category includes cases where a living person's phone call is answered by someone who the caller later learns has been dead for some time. In these instances, the intended recipients of the call typically assure the caller that they were present at the time but say that their phone did not ring, or that no one was at home at the time the call was made.

A fourth category includes unexpected calls that coincidentally address the issue the recipient wants to talk about. This suggests the involvement of some form of telepathic communication between the dead and the caller, though the caller is not aware of being 'used' by the deceased to convey the message.

WISH YOU WERE HERE

Connie lost her teenage son Jason in 1994, when he was killed in a crush at a Pink Floyd concert at the JFK Stadium in Philadelphia. A few days later her 21-month-old grandson picked up the phone, which had not been ringing, and began an animated conversation. When asked by his mother who he was talking to he replied, 'Uncle Jason', as if she should have known who would be calling. But when he handed her the receiver there was no sound and, curiously, no operator asking her to hang up. Seven years later, Connie's grandson was playing on his computer when the title of the Pink Floyd album *Wish You Were Here* appeared on the monitor in a stream until it filled the screen. On another occasion, the boy sat up in bed and held a conversation with his 'uncle', telling his mother and grandmother details of Jason's childhood that he couldn't possibly have known.

CRASH CALL

One Sunday morning, Jerrod Zelanka was surprised to receive a phone call in the early hours from a woman who was clearly in some distress. Although the voice was faint and the woman's weeping made it difficult for him to hear what she was saying, Jerrod thought he recognized it as his friend, Leah Jean Ash. The only words he could make out were 'I'm at the bottom of a dark hole' – then the line went dead. When he tried to return the call, the number was identified as withheld. Jerrod and a friend went in search of Leah and two hours later discovered her body, with that of a companion, at the bottom of a drainage canal. It appears that Leah and her friend had been killed when their three-wheel all-terrain bike plunged down the bank. The curious thing was that neither girl had been carrying a mobile phone.

BEFORE THE FUNERAL

Lesley Hanafi was woken early one February morning by the phone ringing. When she answered it she was shocked to hear her mother, who had just died after a debilitating illness. Her mother sounded chirpy and told her daughter that she felt much better. As the call ended, Lesley noticed that the bright sunshine which had filled the room only moments earlier had faded to the dull grey light of a winter dawn. Lesley still held the receiver in her hand. The call had been so real that she now wondered if she should call off the funeral and cancel the caterers!

OTHERWORLD SERVICE

A lady who wishes to be known only as Jenny told Heathcote-James of the morning her late husband had spoken to her through the radio.

It was 5am and she was having trouble sleeping. The radio was on and tuned to the BBC World Service when the music faded and her husband's voice came through clearly, saying, 'Jenny, are you awake?' She replied that she was and he asked if she was all right. She answered and it was at that moment that she realized she was talking to the radio. She became alarmed; a cold shiver ran through her body and brought her out of the calm, semi-conscious state in which her husband had been able to communicate with her. The music faded back in and his last words were lost.

Three true facts

Such calls are impossible to corroborate, of course, but occasionally an individual will have the presence of mind to 'test' the caller. If this provides validation that the call is genuine, it becomes more difficult to doubt other such calls.

Sharon Stables lost her 22-year-old son after he suffered a brain haemorrhage. She experienced various phenomena which gave her the confidence to contact him by simply relaxing into a receptive state and asking if he was there. Soon she heard his voice and they had a conversation, but still she wondered if she was imagining the whole thing. So she asked for some form of proof and her son told her that he was with a friend who could tell her three things that only he and the friend's mother knew about. When Sharon contacted the friend's mother she was able to confirm that all three were true.

You have mail

If ghosts can drive cars, pilot airplanes and move objects around your home, could the more computer-literate spirits communicate with their friends and loved ones via email, even after their account has been terminated, so to speak? There are several instances of emails that have been sent after the account-holder's death, but the majority of these are spammers who have hijacked the account-holder's information, or they are automated reminders from social networking sites urging users to 'reconnect' with their deceased 'friends'.

However, when 32-year-old Jack Froese died suddenly of a heart attack in June 2011, his friends and family received posthumous emails they believe could only have been written by him. Five months after his friend's death, Tim Art received an email in the terse language that was typical of Jack and on a subject Tim had discussed with him just days before his death. The subject heading was 'I'm Watching,' and the text of the message read, 'Did you hear me? I'm at your house. Clean your f***ing attic!!!'

Art was convinced his friend had written it because, shortly before Jack's death, the two friends had been in Art's attic and Jack had teased him about the mess.

Jack's cousin, Jimmy McGraw, also received a posthumous email in which Jack referred to an ankle injury that Jimmy had suffered after Jack's death. Jimmy believed it was Jack's way of reassuring his cousin that he was all right.

Doubters would say that the emails were a cruel hoax perpetrated by someone who had hacked into Jack's account, or perhaps they had been set up by Jack before his death, using a site such as Dead Man's Switch which allows subscribers to write emails for a group of preselected recipients. These emails are automatically sent after the author's death. But Jack Froese had no idea that he was going to die; his death was sudden and unexpected. So it may be that he is among the first ghosts to have got into the machine.

THE VOODOO DOLL

They say it's never a good idea to take employees or servants for granted, and exploiting or abusing them is bound to invite trouble.

Thomas Otto and his wife were, by all accounts, an unpleasant pair. They built themselves a charming house in Key West, Florida in 1898, but treated their servants so badly that one maid took a singular form of revenge. She gave the couple's young son, Robert Eugene, a straw doll. It was about 90 cm (3 ft) tall, dressed in a white sailor suit and carrying a toy lion. It was a curiously ugly thing, but the child took a shine to it immediately and his parents didn't suspect that the maid had an ulterior motive. But she was practised in the art of voodoo and had placed a curse on the doll.

Within days of naming the doll after himself, the child was heard talking to it and answering back in an eerily querulous voice. Then the unexplained disturbances began. Objects were thrown around, items broken and liquids spilt. The boy blamed all these occurrences on his doll. Nobody believed him, of course, but one night his mother rushed to his room after hearing a disturbance and couldn't open the door. She could hear her son screaming, furniture being overturned and objects being thrown against the walls, but although the door to the child's room was never locked his mother couldn't prise it open. Then suddenly the door gave way and she burst in to find Robert quaking in his bed, surrounded by broken toys. He could only utter one sentence over and over as he pointed a shaking finger at the doll at the end of his bed. 'Robert did it.'

'Robert' the doll was immediately confined to the attic and nothing more was said about the incident. But after the parents died, their son inherited the house and recovered the doll, which passers-by reported seeing moving by itself from one side of the upstairs window to the other.

Robert married, but his wife would not tolerate her husband's obsession and had the doll returned to the attic. When Robert heard about this, he flew into a rage and retrieved it, giving it a room of its own so that it could look into the street and shout abuse at passing children. When accused, Robert denied he was behind it all and insisted that he had removed the doll to the attic only to find it back in its rocking chair by the window when he next looked. And still the sightings of the doll continued, with local residents claiming they had seen it moving when there was clearly no one else visible at the window.

By this time, neighbours and family members were openly discussing the possibility of having Robert committed to an asylum, although more than one person attributed the malevolent influence of the doll to the former servant and suggested burning it to lift the curse. But no one was courageous enough to risk incurring Robert's rage.

When Robert died in 1972, the doll remained in the house and was claimed by the young daughter of the new owners, who were blissfully unaware of the influence it had exerted on the previous occupants. But they soon learnt it was not as innocent as it looked. The girl accused the doll of 'torturing' her, and thirty years later is allegedly still too traumatized to tell precisely what happened to her in that house when she was alone with the voodoo doll.

The house in Key West is now a guest house, but its occupants don't sleep soundly and several of them have complained of hearing someone or something pacing the floor. The doll has been put on display in a glass case in the local Fort East Martello museum. This building has since witnessed all manner of poltergeist activity, including lights turning on by themselves and a soft tapping on the glass case as if 'Robert' is asking to be released.

6

LIVING WITH THE DEAD

Ghosts are everywhere these days. They haunt the internet, and there's a paranormal reality television show on almost every channel. But if you want to get up close and personal with the spirit world there's only one way you can be certain you are communing with the dead – and that is by consulting a medium. It's the medium's job to encourage the dead to share their secrets. Mediums also act as interpreters of verbal and visual messages from beyond the grave.

So how do mediums discover their abilities and develop the talent to tune into the spirit world at will? How do they overcome their own fear of communing with the dead and, most important of all, how can they tell that what they see and hear is real and not a figment of their imagination?

BECOMING A MEDIUM

June Mayfield (real name withheld by request) is a professional medium. She gives regular readings at psychic fairs and at a complementary health centre near her home in London, England. This is her account of how she became a medium.

'I'd always been interested in the paranormal, but it wasn't until I experienced a number of life-changing events that had been accurately predicted by another psychic that I seriously considered exploring the possibility that I might have some degree of psychic sensitivity that could be of practical help to people.

'I was very fortunate in having a psychic friend

who was very experienced and who was willing to teach me. So I felt confident to open up and to allow whatever impressions came through, knowing that he was there holding my hand, so to speak. He was also the most grounded and calm person I knew, so I felt safe, which is very important when you first begin to trust your intuition and invite whoever might be "out there" to communicate with you. He taught me the importance of closing down and protecting myself so that I am in control at all times and not in danger of being overwhelmed, because once you open up and are receptive to the more subtle impressions in the ether, you can attract anyone from the other side who wants to communicate with their loved ones. It's a bit like being a beacon in the darkness. You have to link in with one spirit and not be distracted or tempted to help them all.'

FINDING SPIRIT GUIDES

Once June had been taught to attune herself to the unseen presences who wished to communicate with her or her clients, she needed to establish a connection with her own spirit guides. This would enable her to ask for their advice whenever her friend wasn't present, or when she needed re-energizing or healing after a particularly exhausting session.

'Clients come with all their anxieties and some with

debilitating ailments which can drain the medium of vital energy, so I often need to replenish the life force after a few readings.

'My guides come in various forms, some human, some animal, but I don't analyse why they take those forms or whether they are projections of an inner aspect of my personality or an external spirit. It's not important to me what they are, but how effective they can be in assisting me to help the people who come to me for guidance, or to rid them of something that has attached themselves and is draining them of the life force. The client won't be aware of what it is that is causing their chronic symptoms such as headaches, or leaving them feeling depressed and weak, but I can often see it. And when they leave they will often say how much better and more positive they feel, or that they feel as if they have been relieved of a burden they'd been carrying.

'The quality of the energy associated with these leech-like entities is quite different to the energy that surrounds a spirit which accompanies a client to a reading because it wants to communicate something of importance or to simply reassure the client that there is no need to grieve or worry about the future. Some of those that attach themselves to the living aren't necessarily bad. They might have died suddenly and not be aware that they are dead, or be confused and living in a dream-like state in which they cling to someone they knew in life who has a strong life force. But these lost, earthbound souls need to be made aware of what happened to them and where they are and to accept that they need to move on.'

WORKING WITH A GUIDE

To connect with her guide, June visualizes a specific scene that she must enter, such as a walled garden or a winding staircase which she descends step by step; with each step, she sinks deeper until eventually she reaches a trance-like state. Visualizing the familiar scene helps to establish a connection with the guide, which will appear as if on cue to answer her questions or to reveal the reason behind something that has been of concern.

'There was a time when I was convinced that a certain problem was going to have a disastrous outcome and everyone I had spoken to about this had told me this situation could only end with the person concerned going to prison. And yet my guide assured me that this person would be given another chance and that I shouldn't worry. He wasn't a family member or a friend, but I was still very worried for him and I couldn't imagine how he would escape a jail sentence under the circumstances, but my guide was proven right and I haven't doubted him since. I believe that the more you trust your guides and also the impressions that you receive from a person that you are asked to do a reading for, the stronger those impressions will become and the more accurate will be your reading.

'During readings, words will pop into my head faster than I could have thought of them, and after I have passed the message on or made a particular observation, I won't know why I said that, so that tells me it's not a product of my imagination. Often I'll pick up an energy around the client just before they arrive and the quality of that energy will give me a sense of what they have come to consult me about. I feel a different energy if they have come about a relationship than I do if they are considering a new job or pursuing an ambition which they aren't sure will be successful.'

GIVING A READING

Readings are not always dramatic and life-changing, but they can be important in convincing non-believers that psychics can see more than the average person. In one reading for an elderly man, June described his two daughters and their personalities in considerable detail and examined how they were coping with various events and changes in their lives.

Another example was when a young woman in a very troubled state came to her for a reading.

'As always, I asked the client not to tell me anything, but simply to answer "yes" or "no" to any questions I might ask,' said June. 'I immediately had the impression that she had been jilted by a man who had left her for someone else and taken her money. I then got one word, "leverage", and that was all she needed to hear. She had something on this man, something that if she told the police would certainly lead to him going to prison for a long time and though she didn't want to use it against him, the threat of revealing it was the only thing that would force him to return the money. So the spirits were telling her to use what she knew to recover what was rightfully hers – and she did so.'

Mediums often feel a vibrant energy around a client that they can 'read', or they describe a sensation similar to having a bucket of water thrown over them. These sensations tell the medium that whatever the client is talking about will have a very positive outcome. But if, for example, June is listening to the client describe a relationship and she doesn't get a sense of a dynamic energy surrounding the client, then she knows that the relationship isn't working. Often she will feel a coldness at the back of her neck, when the spirits are standing behind her, or a light touch of fingers in her hair. It is always a reassuring sensation – it is never unsettling.

THE ASTRAL PLANE

June has a friend who regularly leaves his body at will to explore the astral plane – the non-physical world where the soul is said to reside after death while awaiting rebirth. He tells her that the people he has encountered there are just the same as they were when they were alive. Many are repeating their routine lives in this dream world because they cannot imagine doing anything more or breaking free of their addictions and attachments. Death does not necessarily give them insight, so communicating with these discarnate souls will not necessarily be positive or increase our understanding. Those more advanced souls who have managed to discard their attachment to people and possessions will either have chosen to reincarnate to continue their development, or will have passed on to a higher level beyond human contact.

'I wouldn't go to a haunted house for fun, knowing what I know. You wouldn't go into the jungle and poke around with a big stick to see if anything will come out and bite you, would you? And you don't wander into dangerous neighbourhoods after dark armed with a torch and a camera if you've got any sense. I don't see any point in going exploring unless you know what you are looking for and what you'll do when you find it. Ghosts are just people without physical form and we all know that there are people you wouldn't want to mix with when they're alive, so why seek them out after they've died?

'If there is anyone who wants to communicate with me from the other side I can wait for them to come to me. There is so much danger in dabbling in something you don't and can't ever really understand. It's not that there is a serious risk of being possessed, but rather of picking up attachments and of the psychological damage that might occur if you think you're possessed.

'That is the real danger that none of these ghost-hunters even consider. I left a Wicca group years ago because they were conjuring up all sorts of nature spirits and the people involved in the group were powerful personalities who knew what they were doing. But what guarantee was there that the spirits would do as they were told when they got here? There is no such thing as a tame and submissive spirit. If it has got a mind of its own, how do you know it won't turn on you? And if you can't see it and can't touch it then you can't contain it or put it back in the bottle!'

June says, 'I don't see any value in these paranormal reality shows which seem to be everywhere at the moment. How can these ghost-hunters seriously expect to establish communication with the dead, let alone encourage a materialization, if they clamber all over a supposed "hot spot" with tons of equipment and cables and they can't stand still and be quiet for more than five minutes!

'I recently visited Chartwell, the 500-year-old house that once belonged to Winston Churchill, and as soon as I entered I felt shivers from the residual energy in the room. But once the rest of the touring party came in behind me it dissipated. That's why these shows can't hope to capture anything significant. Communing with spirits is a matter of tuning in and being acutely sensitive to "echoes" in the atmosphere and residual energy in personal possessions. It's not a psychic safari!

'I try not to be too sceptical, nor too trusting either. There is so much nonsense written and talked about ghosts and the spirit world by people who have no personal experience and little understanding of the paranormal. The unknown is part of our world and it operates according to natural laws. The supernatural is an extension of our world, not a world of superhuman powers and demons.'

CONCLUSION

I have spent most of my adult life exploring the supernatural, teaching psychic development and sharing personal experiences of the paranormal with the many mediums, healers, past-life regression therapists and students I have been privileged to work with over the years. I thought I had a fair understanding of what ghosts were and how they fitted into the greater reality that we may glimpse from time to time. But I have been surprised by some of the stories and insights that have come to light during the course of writing this book, obliging me to question my own beliefs and assumptions. Nevertheless, I am still convinced there is nothing to fear 'out there'. In thirty years of practising various methods for attaining altered states of awareness, I have never experienced anything disturbing or felt threatened by unseen, malevolent forces, or even been aware of their existence. Although some people claim to have experienced all kinds of disturbing phenomena, I do not believe there are evil entities waiting to take possession of our bodies or our homes.

As long as we can accept paranormal phenomena as glimpses into an alternate reality – one that does not contradict natural laws, but exists as a non-physical dimension of mind and spirit – then I am confident we

CONCLUSION

may cease to invest myths and shadows with the power to unnerve us. So, if you feel the urge, join a psychic circle or go on a guided ghost tour, but don't lose sleep over what you might see or experience.

Enjoy the journey. I wish you good hunting.

Acknowledgements

The author is indebted to the following for their contributions to this book:
Mike Harris, Taz Thornton, Mick Venning, Simon Jeffries, Ann Sinclair, Per
Faxneld and the Bodhitree Adventure blog.

Bibliography

Austin, Joanne *Weird Hauntings* (Sterling, New York, 2006)

Bradford, Anne *Worcestershire Ghosts and Hauntings*
(Hunt End Books, Redditch, 2001)

Bradford, Anne and Taylor, David *Haunted Holidays*
(Hunt End Books, Redditch, 2002)

Bradford, Anne and Roberts, Barrie *Strange Meetings* (Quercus, London, 2002)

Bathroom Reader's Institute *Uncle John's Endlessly Engrossing Bathroom
Reader* (Advantage Publishers Group, San Diego, 2009)

Fenwick, Peter and Fenwick, Elizabeth *The Art of Dying*
(Continuum, London, 2008)

Heathcote-James, Emma *After-Death Communication*
(Metro Publishing, London, 2003)

Mumler, William *The Personal Experiences of William H. Mumler
in Spirit Photography* (Colby and Rich, New York, 1875)

Ratner, Lizzy and Seth, 'Nightmare On Your Street'
(*New York Times*, 30 October 2009)

Roland, Paul *Hauntings* (Arcturus Publishing, London, 2008)

Roland, Paul *I Remember Dying* (Quantum, London, 2006)

Roland, Paul *The Complete Book of Ghosts* (Arcturus Publishing, London, 2012)

Shillito, Ian and Walsh, Becky *Haunted West End Theatres*
(The History Press, Stroud, 2007)

Internet Resources

www.astralhealer.com
www.californiapsychics.com
www.forteantimes.com
www.paranormal.about.com
www.prairieghosts.com/myrtles.html
www.snopes.com
www.spookyisles.com
www.yourghoststories.com

INDEX